A Different Drummer

A Memoir of Growing Up

Bill Vossler

Bill Vossler Books

Copyright © April 2025 by Bill Vossler

Dedicated to my patient and incredibly helpful writer-wife, Nikki Rajala, whose philosophies, copy-editing, and reviewing skills helped me get the manuscript right. Thanks to *St. Cloud Times* editor Alice Mannette for suggesting I make the columns into a book, and *Gannett Corporation* for okaying it.

Foreword

Ever since I was a kid, I realized I am different. Not in a bad way, though. It started when I discovered in third grade that I was left handed, when I didn't receive the same tool to help me learn to write cursive, like the other kids in class did.

"Oh, Billy, you're left handed," our teacher said. "Yours will come next week."

It never did come, which imprinted in my mind that a lefthander was different.

That summer my new step-dad Walter and his brother Howard taught us to play baseball. When Howard set me up on the right side of the plate for batting, Walter said, "No, Billy is left handed. He swings the bat from the other side."

After that in different venues I would hear that I was a left hander. In sports I heard, "He's a southpaw, a lefty, a wrong-hander." Each comment, I believed, meant others thought I was unusual, even weird. Or when I wrote, people commented that I didn't smear the bottom of my left hand with ink as I wrote, because I wrote vertically.

Then when I read Henry David Thoreau's quote: *"If a man does not keep pace with his companions, perhaps it is because he hears a different drummer. Let him step to the music which he hears, however measured or far away."*

Immediately I knew he meant me: I heard a different drummer. I stepped to a different music. I lived life differently from my peers. Not intentionally, but merely because when activities of any kind intrigued me, I pursued them, and didn't care what others thought.

Because the statements about lefthandedness were not hurtful or demeaning, I didn't feel poorly or react at all and became used to hearing my name and simply thinking it was no big deal that they were talking about me, because I was different. So being left handed I felt unique, and different. Unusual. And I liked that.

I did many different things that other kids didn't: I delivered newspapers every day for nine years--see *Freedom*--sat at customers' tables after supper talking with them while collecting for the paper; spent time with teachers in their homes; worked as projectionist for the Dakota Theatre--see *Ervin Attends The Movies;* and as a seventh grader began to write, penning words on sheets of typing paper torn in half. In high school I wrote a novel titled *Forward Into Time*, based on the movie *The Time Machine*, which I projected at the theater.

I wrote short stories and handed them out to classmates in school to get their opinions, and passed them out in church Sunday mornings, where I suggested that my in-church classmates should read them during the sermon, because the preacher's words would be the same that Sunday as every week: *You suffer from the original sin of Adam and Eve, and today you just continue to be another rotten sinner.*

Losing my father when I was 3 had a massive effect on my life. Shortly after Nikki and I married, she said, "Do you realize you mention your dad in almost everything you write?" In this book I wrote about my dad and feelings in *Life Without Father*, and *A Child's War Story*.

Other pieces in *A Different Drummer* include my short stories, *The Life and Death of Chrissie Chrysops*, and *Some Kind of Love Story*.

Growing up in a Germans-from-the-Ukraine enclave of 1,288 people--99% GfU--with an unusual culture, helped me realize, as I moved out into the wider world, how different that culture was, and how it made me different. Check *Learning to Forget*, about the only time I saw my Vossler grandparents, a piece published in United Airline's *Hemispheres* magazine, twice. Also read others in this book, like *It Takes a Village, Paranoid About Praise*, and tell more.

I wrote about my love of nature in *Water, Nature's Magic Elixir, The Strength of the Land in Me*, and *The Fullness of the Empty Lot*.

In later life I continued to hear a different drummer: teaching on the Standing Rock Sioux Indian reservation--see *The Saga of Alfred* and *Meeting American Indians*.

I bought a bookstore and opened a second one, keeping both of them open while teaching full time. I wrote about those businesses in *Running a Bookstore*. All of these experiences affected me in different ways. Thus the "different drummer."

I also received this Smithsonian letter below identifying a dozen fossils I found in the empty lot across the street, and sent to them. Their IDs indicated I'd dug up molar teeth of an ancient camel, incisor of an extinct horse, and a bison molar.

```
Dear Mr. Vossler:

    Your request for identification of fossil specimens is hereby
acknowledged.  I have taken the liberty of numbering them in order
to distinguish them and submit the following information:

1-4.  Molar teeth of extinct horse, probably Equus complicatus.

5.    Incisor tooth of extinct horse, probably Equus complicatus.

6, 7. Molar teeth of an extinct species of Bison.

8.    Distal end of metapodial, probably horse.

9.    Proximal phalanx, probably horse.  Note that number 9 articu-
      lates fairly well with number 8.

10.   Distal end of phalanx of horse?

11.   Distal end of metapodial of artiodactyl.  Not right for deer,
      moose, elk or Bison; possibly camel?

12.   Possibly piece of skull of large artiodactyl-like Bison, from
      frontal region near base of muzzle.

    A word of explanation:  The metapodial is the foot bone just
below the hock, and the phalanges (singular, phalanx) are toe bones.
The term distal refers to the end of a single bone, or a bone in a
series, farthest from the body.

    All of your specimens are from Pleistocene (Ice Age) deposits.

    This material is being returned to you under separate cover.
When you receive it, please sign, date, and return the white copy of
the invoice in the enclosed envelope which requires no postage.

                         Sincerely yours,


                         Nicholas Hotton III, Acting Curator
                         Division of Vertebrate Paleontology
Enclosures
```

I also tell more recent stories, like *Experiencing Caribbean Culture*, or *Adventures With Crotalus Atrox*, a rattlesnake.

I could go on and on--but instead, I'm hoping you will.

4

Learning to Forget

This piece was published in Hemispheres *magazine, United Airlines' in flight--twice, the second time named one of the best in the previous 10 years. They claim to print only "the best writing in the world." Pretty heady for me.*

"O teach me how I might forget," lamented Romeo after slaying Tybalt. Or was it Macbeth after doing away with Duncan? Or was it...well, I forget. That happens to me more often nowadays: mental trains of thought clacking by in a blur (what were we just talking about?), or shunted momentarily onto sidetracks (where are my car keys?), or derailed permanently (my first girlfriend's name?).

No great surprise, of course, with the hurly-burly of daily life piling up the flotsam and jetsam along with the increase of years. Experts say our burdened brains simply can't keep everything available for remembering or else the gray matter would seize up like an overheated automobile engine. The experts also say it is healthy to forget. Otherwise the trickle, not to mention the raging rivers, of pain and disappointment and anger endemic to living would become an ocean in which many of us might drown.

But some things I cannot forget, no matter how I strive. Like the memories of those sad and gentle brown eyes that my mother bade me put aside many years ago.

"Just forget them," she said. Forget that beleaguered, elderly couple standing behind their black porch railing, beckoning me with their bent fingers. And because I was only 7, and had been told to forget, I did forget.

But my dreams were suffused with memories of their sad faces. Tell me, how do I undream or teach my memory to forget? Lord knows there is much to forget--the embarrassments, transgressions, and stupidities my flesh has been heir to. Oh, to simply snap my fingers. Begone! Like the time I sneezed a mouthful of milk over my newly-met dream woman. Two hundred delighted witnesses in the college commons roared. The milk dripped off her blond curls onto her banana cream pie. Oh, to forget that!

A different fall day an elderly couple halted my younger brother and me with a mournful cry. At 7 and 5, we were old enough to fetch jars of fresh milk from our cousins' cows every day.

Mom had warned us to avoid one particular house on our route, the one with the black porch railing near the water tower. Obediently, we always skirted past it on the far side of the street.

On this day, the cries of an old couple on the porch of that small white house stopped us. "*Boova,*" they croaked plaintively in our Germans-from-the Ukraine dialect, beckoning us with their fingers. "*Boova. Com doh a bissel.*" Boys, come here a bit. They jingled shiny coins and held them out to us, and seemed so sad that we forgot Mom's warning and rushed across the street and up onto their small porch. The woman piled coins in our palms and then disappeared inside and reappeared with a plate heaped with fresh-baked cookies.

Soon we were sitting on their laps, clutching coins in one small hand, stuffing cookies into our maws with the other, while the man and woman stared at us with their sad brown eyes and desperately clasped their arms around our midriffs. While holding me, the man heaved back and forth in his rocking chair, creaking the porch boards, while he laughed and ruffled my hair.

Then the woman crushed me to her warm, ample bosom. She grimaced, moaning, kissing me wetly as she sobbed, crooning, "*Boova, boova, mina gloyna boova.*" Boys, boys, my little boys.

Finally, bored and cookie-sated, we wrestled loose. The old woman glanced wildly around, then thrust the cookie plate at us. Two cookies skidded off and shattered into myriad pieces. When I shook my head, the woman grabbed her husband's arm and said shrilly, "*Gelt, gelt, Schnell, schnell!*" Money, money, quick, quick! But we clomped down the steps and ran onto the street.

I glanced back. The woman leaned heavily against a porch post, her shoulders jerking, shiny trails glistening down her creased cheeks. The man sat stone-still in his rocking chair, staring ahead.

At home, I showed Mom the booty and recounted our adventure. She shrieked, snatched the money from my hand, and raced into the bathroom. The coins clattered into the toilet bowl amidst flushing water.

Grim and red-faced, she shook her finger at me. "I said stay away from them! Don't ever go there again. Forget about them! Do you understand?" I nodded.

Not long after, they moved away; *marravarich* (stinkweed) grew rampant in their yard. The door canted on one hinge. The porch floor rotted through. We no longer went for milk, and over the years the sheer weight of other memories silted this one under.

Like a dinosaur bone, the incident was deeply buried, but not gone. As years passed, the sharp edge of some other memory would unearth a bit of the bone, but I immediately reburied it. Until 30 years later, when I was home on a visit, alone with my mother.

I was glancing out the kitchen window, fondly remembering days playing baseball, digging up Indian artifacts, building snow forts; and then my eyes fixed on the water tower.

The incident with the old couple, and Mom's reaction, rushed back with staggering intensity. I saw the old woman's shaking shoulders, the man staring blankly, Mom's grim face. Why was I supposed to forget about them? And who were they?

At first I hesitated--our family motto was: Painful? Just forget it--but she was happy and more open to discussing the past. So I heaved a deep breath and unearthed that dinosaur bone.

Mom stiffened. "What nice old couple?"

"Oh, you know. The ones I got the money from? The old couple you told me to forget about?"

Her face went white. "What do you mean, old couple?"

"Well, maybe they were only in their late 50s or early 60s, but you know how kids think."

Gruffly, she said, "You don't know?"

The silence stretched on. I stared out the window. The clock ticked loudly. Finally, I figured, I might just as well forget about it.

But I heard her snuffle. When I turned around, tears glistened in her eyes, streaking down her cheeks. In a hoarse whisper she said, "Don't tell me you really don't know."

"I don't. Otherwise, I wouldn't have asked," I added irritably. But truth had already begun to lay a cold finger on my shoulder.

For moments she kept her eyes closed, lips trembling. Finally she choked out, "They were---that was Jacob and Christina Vossler."

I looked at her blankly. She said, "Your father's mother and father. Your grandparents."

"My grandparents," I whispered. Slowly I sank into a chair, head swirling, heart thudding.

"You never knew they were your grandparents?" Mom rasped in an awful voice.

I stormed from the house and sped recklessly to the lot where their house had once stood. I parted the waist-high weeds, and there where they had once held me in their arms, I sank to the cold ground and cried. I cried for the love and the lives that had been forfeited from me. Like the Montagues and the Capulets, our families had warred since before my birth. My father had abandoned us when I was 3, and I had never gotten to know his side of the family. In fact, I had been pressed to forget about them.

And I had. It seems preposterous now, but for 30 years I had forgotten all about my relatives. The Vosslers, ashamed of my dad, had never contacted me. And I, fearful of upsetting my family's equilibrium, had never contacted them.

Nothing can remedy the loss of my grandparents in my life. They have disappeared irretrievably. And how can I forget that?

How can I forget that my step-father, as I later discovered, drove that gentle old couple away from our house time after time as they walked up in their Sunday-best to exercise their grandparental rights? How can I forget the complicity of my mother?

For years, the bitterness of those betrayals burned inside me, as I tried, as Henry King wrote, to "Learn the hateful art, how to forget." My mother and step-father were not cruel people, I thought; they did their best. But with the preventable loss of my grandparents, my parents' best had not been good enough.

One morning years later, after a fight with my wife, as I lay in her arms, I realized I could not remember what our fight mere hours before had been about. How had I forgotten? After Nikki reminded me, I realized: Forgetting is only the last step, dependent first on forgiving--forgiving ourselves for our part in the fray and theirs. Forgive and forget. It is not coincidence that forgive is first, followed by forget. One frees us to do the other.

And so, with time and hard work, I eventually forgave them all--my step-dad, my mother, and, especially, myself. I dimmed, extinguished, and then forgot the fire of anger.

Now whenever I make the long trip back to the graveyard where my grandparents are buried, I kneel beside their headstones and sometimes sing softly, sometimes speak a few words to each of them as I lay a bouquet of flowers on the graves of Jacob and Christina Vossler.

One bouquet for each--of forget-me-nots.

Life Without Father

Most of all I remember that last hug.

Losing a father at any age is difficult. But the confusion and pain are compounded for those who lose a dad while young. My war-hero father, Julius J. Vossler, walked out on us when I was 3.

After the divorce he drove us from Billings to my parents' hometown. I remembered a troubling incident from that trip, and years later when I told my mother, she blanched and said, "You couldn't remember that!"

But I did. Perhaps the poisonous emotional atmosphere between my parents sensitized me to remember that memory.

I have three other memories of him. I'm standing on the worn linoleum floor while my dad hugs me from behind. I snuggle back against his warm chest while he kneels and speaks softly over my shoulder, his breath tickling my ear. I luxuriate in his touch, amidst the heady tang of whiskey.

He flips a small football into the air, grabs it, and sets it nose down on the linoleum, his finger on top,. "Kick," he says urgently. "Billy, kick the ball!"

I'm afraid I'll kick his hand, so I just stare at the ball. He flips it in the air once more and starts to announce the game, his voice rising higher and higher, saying *the clock is ticking down the last seconds of the game, fans, no time outs remaining, Billy Vossler barks out the signals, hut hut hut, say hut* he says, and I squeak out "hut."

He snatches the football, sets it on the floor, says *Billy Vossler eyes the goalposts, the ball is down, he kicks--kick!* he says--and I close my eyes and I kick, and he says *it's up and and and it's good, it's good! Vossler wins!* as the ball knocks down Mom's knickknacks.

My father whoops and hollers, patting me on the back, until Mom rushes in and spots the broken knickknack, and screams. I start crying because she's angry with me, while my father hugs me.

Another memory comes from stopping me with his car as I am walking to school on a cold and snowy day. I was six. He had a woman with him. He said, "Hi, Billy, I'm your father," which triggered a cascade of emotions that brought tears to my eyes, and questions that I'd harbored ever since he left: Where have you been? Why did you leave? What did I do wrong? Why don't you love me? But they were too huge to ask.

I wanted to leap through the window into his warm arms, but I didn't do that either. He promised me a two-gun holster set for Christmas, and I told him to put it behind the door of the white cabinet in the basement.

"White cabinet," he said, "got it."

But he didn't.

When I was 9 and on my way to school he stopped me again. He said I'd grown so big he hardly recognized me. His words so overfilled me with churning emotions that I couldn't respond. As I watched his car drive away, and his brake lights blink on and then off, I didn't realize I would never see him again.

That is the entire pantheon of memories I have of my dad.

In daily life, I was constantly reminded of my loss by the most innocent occurrences, as when my second grade teacher asked what my father did for a living, or the Father's Day project we did in fourth grade--and the word "father" itself which exposed a space in my brain where a great sea had once lapped the shores, but had now gone dry. And I always felt left out, and different.

And forever the eternal hope: will he be here this Christmas? Or Thanksgiving? Or Father's Day?

I mean this to remind you that if you still have a father, thank your lucky stars. And be sure to tell him over and over again that you love him, as many times as there are pinpricks of light in the nighttime firmament.

And don't ever forget to hug him.

This is my father, Julius Vossler, in his service photo, the first one I ever saw of him, when I was 40.

A Child's War Story

Rarely are 12-year-old girls named as heroes during wartime. But let me tell you about one that was--and a soldier, a hero, two people to whom I owe debts of gratitude that can never be repaid.

The story began on a black moonless night in late November, 1944, when a U.S. Army contingent slipped behind enemy lines in France to blow up a German ammo dump. The leader of that nighttime raid was an American soldier whose Army nickname was "Nazi," because he spoke flawless German.

That soldier was my father, Sergeant Julius J. Vossler. Raised on a farm in McIntosh County, North Dakota, a hotbed of Germans-from-the Ukraine, his first language had been the German of the area.

In the local *Wishek Star,* he detailed the battles he had fought, capturing St. De and Stiege, France, and then, he wrote, "November 29, 1944, we, of B Company of 409 Infantry Regiment were called upon to sneak through German lines and destroy an ammunition dump. Me, being the only one who could speak German out of my company, my captain ordered me to take the lead. Three men volunteered to go with me."

"We said goodbye to the rest of our buddies. I thought that would be my last mission because we didn't have a chance. So (that night) we jumped off, and got to the edge of Schletstad, France."

Instead of imminent danger of death, they were unobserved and "destroyed the ammunition dump without any trouble."

Just after midnight they headed back toward their unit. "At a mile away from the rest of the company of 180 men, I contacted my captain and said the mission was completed. At 0100 we joined."

But the elation was short-lived. "We were ready to sleep when hell popped loose. The Germans blew the river bridge, isolating us from our tanks for support. Their tanks laid the lead to us. We fought for four hours..."

At the end of that time, only 17 of the 180 Americans remained alive. "By 0600 o'clock that morning, we ran out of ammunition, so there was only one thing left to do: give up."

As prisoners they were forced to walk for three days and nights, he says, with nothing to eat or drink, until they reached Stalag 12A at Leinberg, Germany. "There they interrogated us, took all our clothes away...and tortured me for three hours...because they thought I was a German soldier who had deserted."

"December 21st they put us in box cars, 50 men in each, and took us to Stalag 3B. We stayed in those cars until December 27th. All we got to eat per man was one-third of a loaf of bread, made of sawdust and spuds, and little water to drink."

Then they were crowded, 400 American prisoners per unheated barracks, where they received two slices of bread and a bowl of carrot soup per day. "On January 27, 1945, we went on a 150-mile march" (sometimes called the Fuerstenberg to Luckenwald death-march.) They passed through Berlin on Hitler Strasse toward Stalag 3A at Luckenwald, where my father escaped.

So ends his newspaper article.

But there is more to the story.

What my father did not mention was how they escaped. He and two other prisoners ripped out electrical wire from the barracks wall and subdued guards. After crossing Germany, they connected with the French underground in Alsace-Lorraine, who hid them in a root cellar, where that girl of 12 risked her life--and her family's--daily, bringing food and water for weeks until they could be repatriated back to Americans.

My family historian brother Ron, tracked down the girl-now-woman 50 years later in Alsace-Lorraine. On his recording of her, I can hear her panic in her screams. She thought the real Nazis of the past had come back to punish her for aiding those American soldiers so many years ago.

World War II, of course, produced many heroes--but certainly this man, and this girl, were two of them.

Super-Secret Agency Helped POWs Escape

I enjoyed combining my research of MIX-X with what I know of my father's escape and travel through 410 miles of war-torn Germany.

Shivering with cold, weakness, and fear in the poorly heated room, my father, now a prisoner of war, SSgt. Julius J. Vossler, duty parcel officer at *Stalag 3B*, watched for his opportunity with slitted eyes. His ration-weary captors, searching POW comfort packages for contraband, were distracted by American POWs offering the Nazis cigarettes, so Julius saw his chance to slip two "loaded" packages into the inspected pile.

Minutes earlier, Julius had spotted the telltale crooked stamps indicating packages that contained more than merely cigarettes and coffee. Perhaps even a "super duper" package containing materials specially ordered by the prisoners of his *stalag*: a camera, photo enlarger, chemicals, photo paper for making identity photos and passes, printing supplies, map pieces in playing cards, radio transmitters in baseballs, and compasses, all to aid prisoners to escape. His heart beat faster; would this have something for him?

Everything listed was provided by a little-known U.S. agency called MIS-X, or Military Intelligence Service-X, whose single-minded goal was to help captured Americans escape Nazi *stalags*, evade the enemy in hostile country, and get back to friendly lines.

MIS-X planned for escapes even before POWs were captured, teaching escape and evasion methods along with MIS-X letter codes and code names, to two soldiers from each battalion. If captured, they were to report to the camp's Allied commanding officer, then write a coded message to a family member or friend.

POW letters with the red or purple German postmark and swastika were easily detected by the U.S. postal system. Letters from

POW code users were flown daily to MIS-X, steamed open, decoded, reinserted, and sent on to the recipient.

Coded letters smuggled information out of the camps, but also relayed information back to the POWs.

The MIS-X process worked because POWs were allowed "comfort" parcels from home, though Red Cross parcels were never used, because they were so precious that the powers-that-be didn't want to destroy that huge advantage. Instead, MIS-X created their own fictitious relief agencies, like The War Prisoner's Benefit Foundation and Serviceman's Relief.

When his chance came, Julius snatched the packages. Suddenly, something inside one clinked, echoing ominously loud. His heart leaping into his throat, Julius glanced at the guards.

But the Germans, reveling in their good fortune of real coffee, hadn't heard the noise. With a sigh of relief, Julius surreptitiously slid both packages into the "inspected" pile.

When he had a chance to open the packages, he discovered just what he needed: German money, a pistol, and a deck of cards where each card had part of a map of Germany.

In order to escape, he and another man had to kill a couple of German guards, and then get out.

Of 85,000 U.S. POWs, only 737 made it back to friendly lines. Most, including my father, wouldn't have succeeded without escape and evasion kits secreted inside comfort packages.

The Germans had suspicions, and found some contraband during routine package examinations, but much got through.

As Lloyd Shoemaker writes in ***The Escape Factory***, "MIS-X was an ultra-secret agency whose finances and activities were scrupulously concealed even from government and military inquiry."

Which they were. Five days after World War II ended, all information about MIS-X was burned, the buildings bulldozed, and trees planted in their stead.

As a result, much about MIS-X and its operations will never be known; what is known that the anonymous men and women of MIS-X made a difference: their work brought hope and aid to captured American servicemen during World War II

And life to others. In July, 1946, I was born.

Learning To Count

My mother was a brave woman, moving from Billings to her home town of Wishek, North Dakota, with three little boys, 5, 3, and 1, after divorcing my father in 1949.

Unable to afford a babysitter, she tapped relatives and friends to take care of us. Judging by stories I heard later of my behavior, I must have been a little hellion. Which may explain why many different people babysat us.

When our neighbor, Mrs. Wagner, babysat us, she made the mistake of giving each of us an ammonia cookie. Yum!

Or rather, the mistake was showing me where the cookies resided--in the bread drawer. While she was occupied with my brothers, I sneaked into the kitchen, opened the drawer, pushed back the cover, and grabbed a handful. Yum Yum.

She discovered my larceny next time she stepped into the kitchen, as I'd left the drawer wide open. She never sat us again.

Then Uncle Otto and Aunt Ella. Years later when I was visiting, Ella led me to the stairs leading up to the second floor, showing me holes I'd made pounding in nails with my uncle's hammer. Just being helpful.

When asked how she liked babysitting us, Grandma Fetzer said, "I'd rather chase a herd of wild horses."

But some of those babysitters altered my life forever.

Once I followed Aunt Edna out into the field where cows were grazing. A vehicle was spewing dust on the gravel road running along the field. "What's that?" She asked, pointing at the car.

"A cow," I said.

"No," she said, pointing at the four-footed animal chewing its cud in the field. "That's a cow. That," she said of the vehicle, "is a car. Say 'car.'"

"Cow."

"No, car."

She worked with me until I could say "car," more often than "cow," awakening in me an awareness of the importance of sound.

When I was 4, my cousin Milo was the babysitter. I sat on his lap while we played Monopoly. When our turn came, I grabbed the dice, cold in my hand, and clunked them on the board. Immediately I grabbed our car token, and smacked it down at random, imitating others, saying, "Datika datika datika," one word for each smack.

Milo grabbed my hand. "No, Billy. Look, Here's how you do it. First you throw the dice." He tossed them. "Now, you count the dots on the dice."

I glanced up at him and blinked. What did he mean?

"Look." He grabbed my finger and touched its tip to each dot on the top of a die. "One, two, three," he said slowly, "and then you move the car that many squares. See?" He moved the car. "One, two, three."

Then he touched the tip of my finger to the dots on the second die. "One, two. And then you move the car that many squares again. See? One, two." He moved the car on the board.

Something dawned on me. A surge buzzed in my brain, and suddenly I sensed what he meant. I grabbed the dice and threw them again and touched each dot and counted them as Milo had, one, two, three, and took the car from his hand and moved one, two, three colored squares.

"Yes!" Milo said, "yes!"

I touched the second die, one, and advanced the car one, square. "Yes!" They all looked at me, smiling. I had learned the rudiments of counting.

Milo cleared his throat and said I had moved the wrong direction on the board, so he had me move in the right direction.

Even though we kids were passed around from place to place, it was clear Mom found people who not only babysat us, but cared for us, and taught us.

It Takes a Village

After our family came back from Billings to Wishek in 1949, Mom's hometown saved us.

Word spread about a divorce judge warning Mom that her boys would become criminals if she divorced our father; on the way back my father threatened to kill us by driving us off a cliff; Mom's father refusing to take us in ("We said don't marry him")! Our dad was gone,; Mom was broke; and we had nowhere to live.

Thus began a series of kindnesses as the village looked out for us. Someone offered us a little corner house; the Security State Bank owner offered Mom a job; relatives and friends babysat.

Uncle Henry retrieved truckloads of coal for our furnace; every once in a while Mom would slit open an envelope without a name or return address, pull out a crisp $20 bill--and start crying.

Small things added up too. We took our worn-out hand-me-down footwear to shoemaker Jacob Rattei. After fixing them in his shop smelling of new leather, he gazed at the paltry coins in my palm, rubbed his chin, and reluctantly took a couple of them.

Several men acted as semi-father figures, especially John Ackerman. One day when I was 5, Mom and I were grocery shopping in the Red Owl. As I walked, glancing at boxes of Wheaties, my favorite cereal, I bumped into a pair of huge legs that blocked my path. I paused, bewildered by the gray pants pressed so sharply they could have sliced butter. A man with a kind face knelt and said, "Hello, little boy. What's your name?"

I could hardly breathe. A foreign but wonderful feeling of a man paying attention to me! Tendrils of aftershave drifted into my nostrils. I didn't know what to do. I quailed, and plunged my face into Mom's skirt.

"That's Billy," Mom said, patting my head.

The man said, "Well Billy. Let's try again." His gentle demeanor disarmed me so I didn't resist as he turned me around and tapped my chest with a finger. "What's your name?"

I stuck my fingers in my mouth. He asked again.

"Biw-wy," I said, through my fingers.

"Billy? I heard that you've been a really good little boy."

I flushed with pleasure. He asked how old I was and I muttered five. "Only five?" He said. "My goodness, but you look older. Let me see your muscles."

He felt my biceps, and jerked his hand back. Goodness, I wouldn't ever want to fight with you," he said. "That's for sure."

I could hardly look at him, I was so happy.

"Now what's my name?"

I shrugged.

"You don't know my name?" He said in mock seriousness. "Why everybody knows who I am. I'm John Ackerman."

He grabbed my saliva-filled hand and poked it against his chest, making a wet spot next to his tie. "John Ackerman," he said, tapping my fingers against his shirt. "Can you say 'John'"?

"J-John."

"That's right!" He squeezed my hand. "John. Good!"

I smiled, and hid in Mom's skirts again. "Now you remember that," he said.

Since my dad left, I had never received such steady attention from a man. I froze in fear. What if I never saw him again?

I needn't have worried. For the next 25 years every time I saw him we repeated the little ritual. "What's your name? What's my name? Good. Remember that." Every time, his smile lay like a warm arm across my shoulder, his repetition of my name reinforcing my sense of self.

As the years passed and Mom remarried, the village continued to watch out for us, offering jobs, friendships, caring, without expecting anything in return.

Walter Delzer and Mom (Alma Woehl Vossler) shortly after their marriage. It had to be a monumental undertaking for him to marry a woman with three little kids, 8, 6, and 4.

Drama at the Railroad Crossing

Heavy summer rains had glutted the ditches along the Soo Line tracks. Karo pails on our belt loops bonged as we kicked rocks, hearing them clatter with the joy of a carefree childhood.

I was 7; my brother 5; we were hunting minnows.

Arms spread, I balanced on a rail, counting steps while flying grasshoppers zipped back and forth. Thirty minutes later the sun was a warm arm across my shoulders as we negotiated the great curve, sunlight glinting off burnished rails, smelling sharp sun-hot creosote, and spotting the flash of sunlight off water. We raced to the minnow pond, the pails thumping like quickening jungle drums.

Minnows fascinated us, dark shards of flesh that darted every which way, retreating to the deep, becoming tiny ghostly reflections until curiosity enticed them upward to study us with pinprick eyes. Dozens, perhaps hundreds of them.

Suddenly I sprang at them, and they exploded like a plate shattered on cement. We chuckled. How could they careen helter-skelter at hundreds of miles per hour without any accidents on their underwater autobahn? Nobody turned wrong or braked late.

We tossed our holey catch-pail with a curly white umbilical cord into the water. On the bottom it raised tendrils of mud, and its open maw proved irresistible. A few minnows swam nearby, then darted inside to investigate. Others followed. I yanked the pail out.

"Look at them!" Ron said, wide-eyed.

"Beautiful!" I breathed, pouring them into another pail, watching the minnows speed around and around.

All minnows were alike, I'd thought, until a stickleback thrust its spines into my finger. Carp were pretty, gold with a long dorsal fin; chubs, gold and purple. Gold-green fins of shiners and silver bellies of fatheads made them distinct as my brothers and me.

When we cupped the minnows in our hands, we found they were like a powerful slippery missile. We squealed with delight. Their strength shocked me.

After nabbing more minnows for sliding on our hooks for fishing at Green Lake, we headed towards home. After a hundred yards walking in the middle of the tracks on the ties I heard the shriek of a train whistle. Behind us. Insistent, as though screaming, "Getttt offfff! Getttt offfff!"

Ahead the ditches were brimful nearly to the tracks. We couldn't swim, and were terrified of water. So that was out.

I knew trains created their own gravity, so while standing close to the tracks beside the water while the train roared by, we risked getting sucked under the grinding wheels.

"What do we do?" Ron asked. His eyes were huge.

The lone safe spot was the crossroads near the pond. Where we'd been. Toward which the train was pounding, a third of a mile away. Coming fast. "Run!" I yelled. Ron turned the other direction.

"No!" I screamed. "This way!" I pointed. "This way!"

"The train!"

"We can beat it. Hurry!"

I turned and ran. Toward the speeding train. Waves of water from the pail sloshed down my pants. I shivered. I looked back. Ron stood mesmerized by the beast throbbing towards us. I screamed and ran back. More water sloshed. I tossed the pail away.

"The minnows!" he said.

I grabbed his hand. "Run!"

The crossroads seemed a mile away. The train pounded and roared and throbbed, growing nearer, larger. The ground shuddered.

The train loomed. Fast. Deadly. The whistle screamed wildly. I dragged Ron behind me. Could we make it? The white railroad signs seemed to cross their arms to ward off the blow from the brunt of the train, which would grind us down and under. My heart hammered. The whistle shrieked. The ground shuddered.

I dove onto the crossing, pulling Ron along. The world became thunder and wind ripping at our clothes, and stars dancing behind my clenched eyes. After a minute we sat up.

Ron said, "We lost the pretty minnows!" But not our lives.

The Missing Christmas Gift

Late afternoon one Christmas eve when I was 7, I was practicing the Bible verse I would recite on stage at the Evangelical United Brethren Church Christmas program that evening.

I always suffered from stage fright and struggled to remember my verse, quailing at all the eyes fixed on me, smiling, though I believed they were hoping I would make a mistake so they could laugh at me--or so I thought in my childhood insecurity.

Earlier I had asked Mom if I was too sick to perform tonight would I still get a bag of goodies later?

"No," she said.

"You could bring me one."

"No," she said, shaking her head, knowing what I wanted.

At that moment a hard knock resounded on the outside door. Mom opened the door to the three-season porch, and her heels clicked on the wood floor across to the outer door, which she unlocked, and pulled open. I heard her suck in a deep breath, and in a strangled voice cry out, "What do you want?"

It was dark and with no porch light I could barely see the figure standing in the cold on the front steps.

And then I heard a voice. A man's voice say, "...jackets for the boys." I squinted, but still couldn't see him, as I heard Mom's anguished voice cry, "I don't want them."

The man said something again, so I took a couple of steps closer, but Mom was standing so she blocked my view.

In a high voice she said, "You probably stole them off somebody's clothes line. I don't want them."

The man's voice replied "No I didn't. I bought them." After a moment he said, "Could I see the boys for a minute?"

"No, they're too busy practicing for the program tonight."

Deep in the primal recesses of my brain, the sound of that voice matched another one. Then I remembered that voice. *His* voice. My father's voice, heard three years ago just before he left us. Every day I thought of him. Hoping he would return. And he had!

"Daddy!" I screamed, dropping my Bible. "Daddy!" And rushed to the porch as Mom said, "Just go!" And slammed the door.

Sobbing, my arms outstretched, I attempted to slip around her and grab the doorknob, but she had already locked the door.

"Daddy!" I said. "I want to see Daddy!"

"Ach," Mom said, brushing tears away. "That wasn't your father. What-what would he be doing here? He's gone. That was," she waved toward the door, "that was, just--just somebody trying to sell us jackets, and we don't have enough money for new ones."

I glanced at the door, and Mom, still dabbing with a tissue.

"But it sounded just like him!"

Mom ushered me unwillingly back into the house, asking if I had my piece memorized. Instead I mentally replayed the sound of his voice, and knew it was him. Was he still around? I glanced out the window, but it was dark. I wanted to see him!

Then I remembered church tonight. Surely he would come there to hear me! I would see him then! What a great Christmas gift! I felt relieved.

In church when my name was called I stood, turned, and searched a several pews, looking for him. Mom nudged me. "Get up there now."

On the stage, I could see the entire congregation of our small church, but nobody resembled him. Tears came into my eyes. I blinked them away and sniffled, and began my piece.

Then the big front door of the church clicked. My eyes opened wide and I stopped speaking. A man walked in. I almost screamed "Daddy!" Another man followed him, both hoisting boxes piled with bags of goodies. Neither was my father.

Somehow I bumbled through the rest of my piece, and sat down, still dribbling tears. Later others patted me, thinking I was crying because of my mistakes. But it was because of the Christmas gift I didn't get, a visit and hug and "I love you" from my father.

A Pair of TV Miracles

I saw my first television set at age 8 when my step-dad Walter brought home a blonde wood Hoffman console TV set from Sayler Bros. Hardware where he worked. One of the first in town.

He set it in a corner of the living room, and began running several wires. Then he crawled up on the roof. When I followed him outside, I saw him up there working on an antenna. I had little idea what it all meant, and kids like me in the Germans from Ukraine culture didn't ask adults questions about anything.

Back inside I saw Mom snap a picture of the TV, and I realized this was a big deal. They were excited. But why?

Outside, Walter yelled down to my brother Bob, "Tell Mom to turn it on."

"Tell him it's on," Mom said to Bob. I looked again. Hundreds of little faces missing eyes or noses or mouths covered the screen. But so what? What was all the fuss about?

"Anything showing?" Walter said.

"Just snow," Mom answered.

I peered at the screen. So that was snow. Not heads. What was the big deal with that? We had snow every winter. Why look at it on a screen in the summer?

I heard scuffling on the roof. "How about now?"

"No."

I was about to go across the street and play in the empty lot when a miracle occurred: suddenly real faces of real people sprang into view on the screen of the TV. But not in color. Then Mom turned a dial--and the faces spoke!

"Yes!" Mom cried, "Yes!"

Thus was I introduced to television. Just because our family had a TV set did not mean we kids could watch TV any time we wanted. Sure, we could watch adults shows with Mom and Walter like "I Love Lucy" or "The Ed Sullivan Show" at night, but watching alone was forbidden. Walter had built a new addition of a living room, and we were outlawed from that wood floor.

At school I learned that a few friends watched Looney Tune cartoons on Saturday mornings. And that Raile Implement Co. had a TV--and the business was only kitty-corner across the alley from our house. The problem was that Saturday morning was Mom's favorite time to load us up with basement-cleaning chores. Two choices--do the chores well and quickly, instead of my usual dawdling and whining--or bug out on Mom when she answered the phone or went into another room. That worked exactly one time.

I even started some Saturday morning work early--shocking Mom--so I could rush across the alley to Raile Equipment Co. to watch Daffy Duck and Bugs Bunny.

The first time I went to watch at the dealership I didn't have the courage to go inside. So I stood outside their streaked picture window and watched the blurry action. But I was equally intrigued by the faint classical music that accompanied the action. I knew little of music without words, and these songs made my heart sing.

And then one memorable Saturday morning after I had begun going inside, another miracle occurred: a show came on, introduced by the most intriguing and wonderful music I had ever heard, with a masked man on a white stallion yelling, "Hi-Yo Silver, Away!" while the steed reared up on its hind legs.

I became enthralled by the adventures of the Lone Ranger and Tonto, and doubly hooked on the *William Tell Overture* (still my favorite piece of classical music today).

I figured out what time it started each week, and didn't miss a show--until Mom discovered my "cleaning" wasn't up to par.

Discovering Money

My curiosity with money began at five, when Mom dropped a handful of coins into my palm and told me to get my shoes resoled by shoemaker Jacob Rattei, a half block away. I'd never held money before.

In the shoe shop I happily inhaled the smell of glue and new leather while he traced the edges of my shoes with a dark pen on a piece of shiny cowhide, and snipped out new soles with large shears.

After some magic, he attached the soles to my shoes, handed them to me, and I put them on.

He grinned as he opened my small hand with his large rough one, and picked out a few clinking coins, and escorted me out the door. I could not quite comprehend the transaction.

At 7, I had mostly figured how money worked--we went to a store and found what we wanted and paid for it and took it home. But I couldn't figure out why we put money in the church collection plate. What were we buying? And we never took anything home.

My interest in money skyrocketed when I was 9 and found a five-dollar bill clinging to the top of a *marravarich* plant. I didn't tell Mom, and spent it all on myself, mostly candy--black nibs and halvah--and pinball machines. A heady feeling!

I'd never had money of my own. No allowance, and I never asked mom for any. Sensing how little we had, and none for my foolishnesses. When we worked for others, our parents collected. So the freedom and power of that five dollars made me yearn for more. But how could I get more? Easy--find more lost money!

But no matter how hard I looked, all I found was a quarter and a nickel by the grocery store. Until that spring while planting potatoes I found an old coin--an 1881 Indian Head penny. Suddenly every clod of dirt looked like a hidden coin. Was a stash right here?

Unfortunately, the garden yielded only one more coin, a 1917 Standing Liberty quarter. I was more than disappointed.

When friends asked what those old coins were worth, I decided to find out. About this time my parents signed me up to deliver the *Minneapolis Tribune*.

As though ordained, one customer was a long-time coin collector. "The penny is common, but the quarter… It's an S, or San Francisco mint. Fine condition. Must be worth, mm, 15 bucks."

"Holy moly!" I said. "Where do I sell it?"

Occasionally in change I'd find a rare coin like this 1917 Standing Liberty quarter.
(John Baumgart photo, Wikipedia)

He shook his head. "I wouldn't. Some of those old beautiful coins, miniature works of art really, still circulate, so you could build a valuable collection of them, especially by using your newspaper money."

I took his advice and didn't sell it, because I started using a little money from my paper route for myself.

So each week before paying our newspaper bill we'd buy rolls of pennies and nickels from Security State Bank, searching for rare ones. "Oh, a 1922-D Lincoln! Too bad it's not a plain, worth $100."

"And here's a 1924-D!"

And one day one of the rarest of all, a 1931-S penny. $30!

My collection grew slowly. But we had pretty well cleaned out the town of all rare or semi-rare coins.

What did I gain from collecting coins? Making friends with other coin collectors; realizing the townspeople liked helping us; noting that the amount of coinage in the town was finite; understanding how money circulated, from me, to a store, to the bank, to other people, back to me; the joy of hunting and finding rare coins; the knowledge about coin collecting; and the collection itself.

Most of my coins are gone, but I still get a thrill remembering my first 1881 Indian head penny.

And also today I still check the coins in my pocket for rare ones.

A Fascination With Coins

Money has always fascinated me. At age 9 I found a fifty-cent piece beside the road on my way home while carrying a jar of milk from my cousin's place three blocks away.

A few weeks later I walked into our house to see Mom on the phone. She glanced at me and said, "Just a minute. I'll ask him."

She said Mrs. Boettcher across the street wanted to know why I always walked with my head down. I frowned. Wasn't it obvious? I mean, didn't everybody? "I'm looking for money," I said.

That spring while planting our garden I discovered two old coins. After the Fordson tractor turned another furrow, my job was to jab a slick piece of potato deep in the dirt. As I did that, one time when I pulled out my hand, a round dirt form caught my eye.

I scraped the dirt off, and was shocked to see a penny showing the side bust of an Indian with a headdress.

My vision went black for a second with the surprise, and then the light poured back in again and I realized what my prize was. Mom reprimanded me with a yell of "*Steig oof.*" Wake up and get busy planting or we'll have a blank row with no potatoes--because the tractor was plowing again.

An Indianhead penny I found while working in the garden.

During those early years some of the United State's most beautiful coins turned up in common circulation: Indian head pennies, buffalo nickels, Barber dimes, quarters, and half dollars.

Sometimes I'd spot these miniature works of art in my change after buying a Snickers bar at the Mindt V store, or getting paid for the newspaper. Many were valuable beyond their face value.

That appealed to me--free money if we found some of the rare ones like 1931-S, or 1914-S, or 1955 double-die pennies. So Ron and I began buying rolls of pennies and nickels from Security State Bank with our newspaper money before paying our Star Tribune Company bill each week.

Our eyes were strong enough to determine the date and mint mark of each coin, and a few of minor rarity showed up, so we kept exchanging roles of pennies and nickels. A couple of weeks later we realized we had been searching rolls that we had previously searched, as we recognized very distinctive coins popping up again: a Lincoln penny with a big nick, a bent World War II zinc penny, two buffalo nickels with dates worn smooth.

We needed a method to identify the rolls we processed. Ron, who knew all the ancient Roman emperors in order by heart, suggested using *Senātus Populusque Rōmānus*, "The Senate and People of Rome," or SPQR, as our identifying mark in black on the side of every roll we searched. Adding those letters made me feel adult-like.

The women at the bank indulged us, removing SPQR rolls from the trays of coins they brought out to us, so we wouldn't repeat going through a roll. Customers frowned when the tellers brought out a tray of pennies and said, "No SPQR on these."

That was the first time I realized the number of coins in the bank was finite, because soon most rolls of pennies and nickels and dimes sported SPQR on their sides, and only a few new rolls without SPQR showed up each week. It was a jolt to see a Red Owl cashier pull out a roll of pennies with SPQR on the side, and smash it open.

But the process was working. We were finding semi-rare pennies like the 1931-S, and rare nickels for our collection, as well as a few dimes, quarters, and half dollars, though we couldn't buy many rolls of quarters and half dollars as they were $20 each.

One of my newspaper customers subscribed to the *Coin World*, and I would be welcome to the issues after they finished with them.

Eventually we cleaned out our town of most of the semi-rare coins, and put them into our collection. I collected coins for many years, and sold off my part of the collection when I went to college. It was enough to pay for the entire first year at Valley City State College in North Dakota.

Water, Nature's Magic Elixir

One winter day when I was 10, my cousins and I were playing hide and seek in the -20 degree cold, when my Aunt Esther stuck her head out the door of their farmhouse. I was immediately visible, so she asked me to fetch a package of beef from the screened summer kitchen. I was sullen about it. Why was I always the errand boy? Besides, I wanted to flush out my cousins.

But I was an acquiescent boy. The screen door to the summer kitchen creaked as I stepped inside, and I waited in the gloom for my eyes to adjust. Through the white balloons of my breath I spotted an old egg crate piled with packages, and took the top one. It was solid and slippery in my snow-covered gloves.

As I turned, I noticed a pail nearby, half under an old blue wooden chair with peeling paint. The pail was filled almost to the brim with what appeared to be water. I blinked and stepped closer. What kind of miracle was this? A pail filled with water at -20 degrees below? Unfrozen? Impossible!

I yanked off my glove to dip my fingers into the "water", thinking I would strike solid ice, but when I reached out, the meat slipped out of my hand, and the package clunked onto the floor.

Instantly the water crackled, and turned into a pail full of ice. Solid ice. I was flabbergasted.

When I took the beef inside and handed it to Aunt Esther, I told her what had happened. "Oh, I don't know," she said. "It must have been frozen, and you saw wrong."

I knew I'd seen the freezing actually happen. The underside of my aunt's blue chair must have had dust or minute pieces of wood or even curls of paint on it, which were shaken loose into the water by the vibrations of the dropped chunk of meat, and my feet--creating instant ice. It was an exciting discovery for me in the book of nature's wonders.

Summer Glories

At age 12, one of a multitude of summer glories for me was the sparkling surprise of fireflies.

They shimmered near a small pond across the street from our house at dusk, and they looked as though their dancing pinpricks were bright points of daylight waiting to disappear.

One evening after noticing a goodly number flickering near the marsh in the far corner of the empty lot, I prepared to collect a few specimens. I needed a container, so I stole a large Ball jar and lid from Mom's stores, and Ron kept her busy while I sneaked out with them. Moments later he followed. We tromped through the *marravarrich* (stinkweed) patch in the empty lot. Watching the huge flock of fireflies, some blinked on and off, seemingly in unison, magical, as though connected by wires into an on-off switch.

At that time the first couple of fireflies were easy to catch, slip inside the jar and clamp the lid on. After that, not so simple, because when I opened the lid to add new ones, those already inside wanted out. Surprise!

I considered catching them one by one and tearing a wing off each to keep them in the jar, but that seemed impractical. I tried, but ended up killing half of them, so I quit.

Once 20 or so were captured in the jar, we headed home. Ron kept Mom busy once more so I could sneak the jar into our basement bedroom. A while later we darkened the room, and were entranced by firefly lights, bright as small candles. Great! I thought.

With the jar, I crawled under the bed covers to see if I could read by fireflies. If so, we probably wouldn't get yelled at for wearing out the flashlight batteries. At least during firefly season.

But no dice. Not enough light. And the flickering made reading impossible. We placed the jar on the bureau and watched with delight as they flicked on and off. Then we fell asleep.

The next morning the bottom of the jar was littered with dead firefly bodies. "We forgot to punch holes in the lid," Ron said. "They suffocated."

Each time after that we punched holes in the lid, but overnight they still died. Perhaps because they were prisoners-- which made me wonder what jail would be like. Or too many in the jar. Or no food. Or a combination of each of these.

Later I discovered unison blinking meant they were all males, exhibiting their bright lights to say, "Here! Look at my nice light. Better than Joe's or Tom's or anybody else's. Take me."

I also discovered that the simultaneous blinking told certain female fireflies that they were safe mates of her own species, instead of the predatory type, which would gladly eat them.

For years I believed we had that a rare firefly species blinked in unison here. But eventually I discovered that wasn't true, as only two species of fireflies blink in unison, and neither species lives in North Dakota. So what I saw was an anomaly.

Nowadays I rarely see fireflies. Yet I still remember the joy we felt at participating in their ethereal beauty during those good old days of nabbing fireflies in the empty lot across the street from our house.

Freedom

    I had never considered delivering newspapers until one day in fifth grade when Miss Smiley answered a knock at the door. "Billy," she said, "there's a man here to see you."

    I leaped to my feet, knocking my math book off my desk and clattering pencils to the floor. Classmates frowned and looked at me. My heart thundered. A man! My father was back! Who else? Was he going to stay this time!

    My knees trembled and my hand was slick on the knob as I yanked the door open.

    "Daddy!" I cried. I gazed up breathlessly, expectantly--into the light blue eyes of a stranger. Hot tears filled my eyes.

    He ignored them and introduced himself. He said, "You're Billy Vossler?" I nodded. "How old are you?"

    "T-ten," I said through my tears.

    He looked me up and down. "Close enough," he said. "You start delivering Monday."

    He began to turn away. "Delivering what?" I asked.

    "Newspapers," he said. "Didn't they tell you?"

    No, they hadn't. But that was how my nine-year daily sojourn of delivering newspapers began. Each morning after scraping myself out of my warm cocoon of blankets, I heralded each day with anthems of joy. I rose from the cool dark ocean of our basement bedroom, ate Wheaties, and pedaled pell-mell to the post office for papers.

    Shortly I discovered I wasn't angry at being forced to deliver newspapers; or about relinquishing my profits to the family coffers-- though my friends were aghast. "You give them *all* your profits?"

    Instead, I was euphoric. For over an hour each day I was my own person. Nobody watched me. Nobody told me what to do.

Nobody said I was doing anything wrong, which seemed to be the normal way. Adults didn't control anything I did. I was free!

So I unleashed my imagination--hearing the roar of the Yankee Stadium crowd as I sent a fastball over the right field fence in the bottom of the ninth to win game seven of the World Series.

Or some days I mentally rode my fully-grown *Tyrannosaurus rex* down the street, his great teeth clacking. I felt his great strength lurch beneath me, gouging footprints deep in the macadam, roaring as he spotted a *brontosaurus*.

Or I stood atop a six-mile-high glacier which had once existed on my town, feeling it rumble, scraping slowly along, unearthing fossils, dragging rocks, pressing the landscape down with its incalculable weight.

Anything I wanted to think, without interruption, I could.

In the full splendor of each new morning I slipped into the godlike silence of the cathedral of deserted streets to experience a new facet of nature; glorying in the smells of the burgeoning bright flowers; or marveling at the trills and flutterings of sparrows and chickadees; or feeling cool raindrops on my face, or splashing on the shining avenues; or smelling the acrid bite of burning leaves; or feeling their crunch beneath my bike tires; or hearing the wild wailing witch of a blizzard as it scratched my cheeks with icy claws, sucking out gouts of white breath from my mouth.

Experiencing the new varied beauties of nature daily, how could I not be impressed? How could I not fall in love with nature?

And during those nine years I learned how to deal with people, chatting at the kitchen tables with those old Germans from the Ukraine while I collected their payments, sharing their hobbies of old coins or arrowheads, talk of their children, and their smiles.

Oh, those were golden days of youth, filled with breathless joy. As Dylan Thomas wrote in *Fern Hill*, *And as I was green and carefree...About the happy yard and singing...In the sun that is young once only, Time let me play and be Golden... All the sun long it was running, it was lovely, in the sun born over and over, I ran my heedless ways...*

But I did not realize those days wouldn't last. Those halcyon days were numbered, already in their death throes, and would pass away, never to return, not for me, nor for anyone else evermore.

Playing With Fire

Fall is the season of leaf-burning. Of the multitude of outdoor chores we were required to perform as kids, raking leaves was less offensive. I was out in the nature I loved, glorying in a steady shower of gold, yellow and red leaves twirling down and falling at my feet, forming a colored carpet.

Once I pulled a pile together, I grabbed our curious cat, Booze-towel, and tossed her in. She disappeared momentarily, but within a couple of seconds poked up her head, covered with leaves. It made me laugh. I jumped in the piles and rolled around, the dry smell of dead leaves filling my nose.

I re-piled the leaves, scraped a kitchen match across the wooden handle of my rake, cupped my hand around the flame, shielding it from the breeze, and watched it grow. Made me feel grown up, though I was only 11. Also fun for the latent pyromaniac in me.

I offered the flame to the pile, like other rakers all over town, so the smell of burning leaves was everywhere, and constant. The leaves were crisp, and flared quickly, shooting up a plume of fire, followed by curling smoke that stung my nostrils quick as the strike of a wasp, making me cough.

The sudden powerful blast of heat made me wonder what it would be like to be burned at the stake. Yikes! Enough of that! I fed more leaves into the fire, watching them melt away.

But the smell of burning leaves was a double-edged sword. For some inexplicable reason it tapped into the deep sadness of missing my father, who left us before I was four.

What hidden thread reminded me of him? When we lived in Billings, had he sat me down outside near him while he raked and burned leaves, creating an ancient half-formed memory that struggled to the edge of my consciousness but couldn't break through when I smelled the distinctive odor of burning leaves?

Burning leaves later proved dangerous for me. While renting a farmhouse as a young teacher near Woodworth, I raked leaves into a pile on the small lawn, and dropped a lit match into them. Catching that powerful smell reminded me of missing my father, but also of happier childhood memories of burning leaves.

Once the fire burned out, I scraped the ashes together, checking for embers or flames, and seeing none, went inside. A half-hour later I smelled smoke. I raced outside to find I hadn't done as good a job putting out the fire as I'd thought. Grass near the house was on fire, growing larger as a new wind whipped it out of control.

No hose, so I grabbed a heavy quilt off my bed, and began beating it on the flames. At first I thought I was doomed, but bit by bit, my breath rasping in my throat, after what seemed like hours, I snuffed it out.

To make sure, I poured pails full of water all around, until I was satisfied it was quenched.

After I returned from a date later that evening, my headlights caught scorched grass near the barn. I frowned. I didn't remember the fire going that far.

Turns out the ground had harbored embers that burst into flames after I left. Luckily someone had called the local fire department who doused the fire. For good this time, before it destroyed the barn or house.

To this day, that distinctive smell of dry or burning leaves every fall tumbles me back to relive the memories of those potent days of my youth.

Learning With David and Jane

Like so many youngsters, my early school days often focused on two names: Not Dick and Jane--but classmates David and Jane.

I grew jealous of David in third grade because he always beat me at math flashcards. So I tried to pre-empt him. The second our teacher's hand twitched to flash the card, I blurted out any number that came to mind, hoping to beat David. Unsuccessfully.

I also wanted to impress golden-haired Jane. David did too, which upped the ante. I was as reckless with class questions, flinging up my hand whether I knew the answer or not.

Neither method worked, nor endeared me to Jane. Plus everybody stared at me, frowning. David's correct answers gave him the edge with Jane.

But the pendulum swung back when I brought Jane home to meet Mom.

Holding Jane's warm hand, we marched down the alley to our house while I pointed out chirping sparrows and buzzing red-winged flying grasshoppers while her great blue eyes held rapt on mine. I brought my blonde-haired beauty right up to Mom, laboring in the garden over rows of potato plants. Mom held a Van Camp's Pork & Beans can.

"Hi, Momma," I said. "This is my girlfriend, Jane."

Mom smiled. "Hello, Jane."

Jane smiled and squeezed my fingers. The heat amplified a sharp smell of kerosene. Jane wrinkled her nose and I thought she might dash away. "I do that sometimes," I said inanely.

"What?" Jane said.

"Pick potato bugs."

"Here," Mom said, giving me the can. "Do it right now."

"Want to?" I said to Jane.

She grimaced, considering. She shrugged and peered into the can, and asked how to get those ugly bugs in there.

I said, "Scrape them off the leaves with the can, or with your fingers."

She pulled a face, but curiosity won out. A few minutes later, pink tongue protruding, she seemed a veteran, lifting leaves, nabbing bugs with bare fingers, plopping them into the kerosene and brushing off her hands. She smiled at me.

"This is kinda different," she said in a low voice, "kinda fun." An upwelling of tenderness surged through me.

It didn't last. Back at school she remained mesmerized by David. I couldn't blame her. David was good at everything: lofting steelies into the marbles pot in one try; able to explain difficult concepts, like baseball standings, which I discovered one noon hour as he explained them, with us laying on the floor, our elbows on the open sports section of the newspaper. Then he called me stupid because I hadn't known how baseball standings worked, so all the fourth-grade girls, like Jane, could hear. I was embarrassed.

In return I spread the rumor that he had pooped in the sink in the boy's bathroom. Then Jane seemed to prefer me for a while.

The dizzying pendulum swung back once more during the Halloween party. While working at our desks, David suddenly screeched "Billy's jack-o'-lantern is burning the curtains!"

Whirling around we saw orange tongues of flame licking up towards the ceiling, and smelled acrid smoke. David threw up and open the big window--he knew how to do that too--and tossed my smoking jack-o'-lantern in an arc of colored flame out into the playground. Had he set the sordid affair up, pulling the curtains down into my jack-o'-lantern to start the fire, humiliate me, and turn Jane against me? Whether or not, it worked. For a while.

I regained cachet with Jane in fifth grade during the reptile unit when I brought in the bones of a snake I had dug up in the empty lot across the street, and laid them out sinuously to oohs and ahhs. And the adoration of Jane.

But I grew tired of the back-and-forth, and began to take an interest in a black-haired girl. Both David and Jane moved away in the next year or so, ending the saga of my first girlfriend.

Languages of the Sousaphone

One day in sixth grade I was informed by the band director that I would be playing a tuba. (Later others called it a sousaphone.) I'd never heard of a tuba. Probably small with a tube, like a flute? Or with a bunch of tubes? So I was mildly interested. No one else that I knew of in my class played an instrument.

I was shocked when the director yanked open a wide door and pointed at a huge brass monstrosity twice as big as me laying on a table. I figured it must weigh a hundred pounds. How was I supposed to hold that beast in my lap?

"There's your tuba," he said.

Mine? Could I play it? Or sell it? How could I possibly blow air from the mouthpiece through all the tubes and out the huge bell at the other end?

I was 5'2" and skinny, so I wanted to say, "Maybe you should find somebody bigger?"

"Just try it," he said. "Pick it up."

"Oof," I said. Not a hundred pounds, but 30.

He said to put it on my left shoulder. I crawled into it--the only way to describe it--feeling thin padding against my shoulder, but also a little thrill. This was weirdly different!

He showed me how the three finger-valves worked. I blew into the tuba and was shocked at how easy the air moved through and made sounds. Hmm! I was intrigued. Different and unique!

The first new musical language I needed to learn was how the valves made unique sounds--music. Hold down valves one and three, blow into the silver mouthpiece and get what he said was the double B-flat tuning note. Other valve combinations made low, medium, and high sounds. A second language was of reading the notes, A through G, plus a flat and sharp for each one.

Another veritable cacophony of a new language I had to learn was reading the notes. They all began as circles. Some blank, some filled in, some with straight or squiggly stems on top. Some notes were connected to each other. Then rests settled in amidst the notes. Notes on lower lines were lower in pitch, high ones higher. He taught me the rudiments of written music in that first lesson.

Over the next months I learned some Italian, as words for playing speeds were all in that language: *adagio* meant slow and stately; *moderato* meant moderate; *allegro* was fast, and so on. Some Italian words were abbreviated: MF for *mezzo forte*, or quite loud; P for *piano*, or soft; *rit.* was *ritardando*, or slow down here.

Two weeks later, after several lessons, I was moved up into the senior band, which needed a tuba to help keep time. At first that required my learning only a few notes. Easy. I felt like a king. I loved the challenge, and being the only sixth grader in band.

Slowly but surely, even though I couldn't bring the tuba home to practice--I had to manage that at school--I progressed.

Repeat, repeat, repeat. Seeing how I improved taught me the value of repetitions. Six years later, I earned a highly-superior rating playing a solo at the State Music Contest.

Part of the band, with me in the right sousaphone.

Accidental Goal-Setting

When I was a sixth-grader, I fell in love with basketball. The heft of the ball, the feel of the rough surface in my hands, the instant response to every dribble, the backwards spin of the ball in flight as it flicked off the ends of my fingers, occasionally swishing through the net, called to me from a deep atavistic yearning, whispering, "This is what you were meant to do."

I had found my niche. The game was in my blood.

Only I wasn't very good.

During open gym my embarrassed older brother screamed, "Hit something besides the bottom of the rim!" as I weakly practiced shooting jump shots while his friends rolled their eyes. When I came home red-faced my step-father would say angrily, "Where were you, out running and jumping again?"

Though momentarily discouraged, I always gritted my teeth and soldiered on, jealous of classmates chosen to play pickup games with older kids, while I was ignored.

In eighth-grade Delmar Benkendorf blocked my last-second shot in a phy ed game, then raced to the other end for the winning score. The next day I was demoted to the seventh-grade team, a disaster of epic proportions in my mind. How could I redeem myself against seventh-graders? Pah!

After another year of bench-riding, I had an epiphany. Want better grades? Study harder. Want more newspaper customers? Knock on more doors. Want to be a better basketball player--practice more! Fueled by the lingering burning shame of my demotion, I made a pact to play basketball every day for at least a year. I would make myself into a better basketball player.

Practice sites weren't a problem; time was. Amidst delivering newspapers, odd jobs, other sports, school and church activities, chores at home, my spare time was limited. But I'd made a pact, and every day I managed to take at least 50 jumpers and 20 free throws, in our back yard, at the tennis court, in the armory, in Erv's alley, in odd off-hours in our school gymnasium, the black curtains on the windows drawn tight so nobody would see we were in there.

Even better at my cousin Jim's place three blocks away, we erected two baskets to play full court across the stubbly ground, two 100-watt light bulbs atop each backboard lighting the dark winter evenings. The bulbs cast garish leaping shadows of grotesque shapes on the court of our twisting ballet. The bulbs flickered dangerously if we banged the ball against the backboard--so only swished shots counted, one way to build up our shooting skills.

We shoveled off snow and raced up and down the court, white balloons of breath puffing out as we shot and dribbled with numb fingers. Each game I worked on one of my weaknesses.

But mostly I practiced alone, following a daily "regiment" (as Erv called it) of at least 50 jump shots and 20 free throws, and working on my skills as if I was being guarded in a game--faking, rebounding, shooting bank shots, hooks, scoops--the stuff of which basketball is made. Meanwhile I was filling out, growing stronger.

To my total surprise, that fall of my sophomore year, my coach tapped me to start B-squad games. And the next year--the next year! Far beyond what I'd ever dreamed, as a junior I became a starting guard on a 20-5 varsity team that missed the possibility of the state tournament by one point.

My days of glory.

When I played basketball every day for a year, I was just trying to make the 10th-grade basketball squad. Little did I know that the concepts I adopted then--choosing and setting a goal, working hard, following through, persevering amidst hardship on -30 degree days!, standing firm to the very end--would reverberate down through the years helping me achieve other, bigger goals, the rest of my life.

An Experiment In Smoking

"This one still has lipstick on it!" I cried, brandishing a cigarette-butt prize for my friend Tom and my brother Ron, who both smiled and nodded.

As red herrings, we each clutched a fistful of Popsicle sticks, so when an adult drifted too near, curiosity filling their eyes at our crawling in the gutter on main street of our little town, we arrested their questions in advance by holding up a stick and bellowing, "Look! Another Popsicle stick!"

As a sixth-grader I knew every inch of the empty lot and environs across the street from my house, so the safest place to perform illicit activities was in a small, hidden sandy square created by the placement of six old railroad cars used as grain bins.

My adventure with smoking had been precipitated one early morning before school when my brother Bob and I biked to the post office to grab that day's package of newspapers for delivery. I saw a smoldering cigarette in the gutter, picked it up, inhaled, and held the smoke in my mouth and knocked on the post office window to get Bob's attention. I puffed out a stream of white smoke amidst a fit of coughing. Bob laughed, so I figured I must have looked cool. That triggered the idea of smoking.

Why not? My step-dad did, Tom's dad did, and so did many other adults. So I brought my friend Tom and my younger brother into the experimental fold. Cigarettes weren't a problem. Tom's dad smoked Marlboros, and my step-dad smoked Old Gold, so we figured we had an inexhaustible source. Thus we each stole a pack.

After school each day for a week we pedaled our bikes furiously down four blocks to the boxcars, where we continued with the experiment, lighting up, imitating different ways to smoke, two-fingered as in the movies, or held solely by our lips, or clenched in our teeth, puffing away, coughing and laughing maniacally. Very cool! But we didn't inhale because we coughed too much!

Soon we ran out of cigarettes. Before I could cop a second pack, my step-dad took out his carton of Old Golds one evening and shook it several times, looking puzzled. He peered inside and frowned, gazing accusingly at me. He said, "I was positive I had one more pack left."

Which meant the days of stealing packs were numbered. Tom had the same result with his father, so we were forced to figure out a way to get more cigarettes. Which was why we took to crawling around in the gutter on main street, picking up used butts.

That trove quickly dwindled, as we harvested months' worth of usable butts in just a few days, and replenishing them was a slow process. So we needed something else.

We turned to dried weeds from the empty lot. Lots of them. But they burned furious and fast, and their smoke was acrid and harsh and stung our mouths and if we inhaled, our lungs. After inhaling, we suffered severe coughing jags, which detracted from the coolness I thought we'd been portraying.

Within a couple of weeks of starting, I wondered what I'd been thinking. What was the big deal? Why did adults even smoke? I didn't get it. So I lost interest.

For a while my friend and his brother smoked homemade corn cob pipes, filling them with my pencil sharpener shavings as a tobacco substitute. Soon enough that paled, ending the experiment for all of us.

The Gift of Gifts

When in the sixth grade I received a mere clip-on tie as my single Christmas gift from my parents, I was frustrated and angry. But what can you say to your folks? "Where are the rest of my gifts" would go over like a lead balloon. My friends were getting fun toys, Tonka trucks and International Harvester tractors, sleds, even a bike. Not me. Though I did get one other gift, which I didn't think of as a gift at all--the bag of goodies from church, with an orange, a ton of peanuts, and way too few sweets.

I had started delivering newspapers a year earlier--*Minneapolis Tribune, Grit,* sometimes *Minneapolis Star*--at which time my parents asked how much I was earning each week. Sensing where this was heading, I was smart enough to lie, because with money tight, they would require all my profits to be placed in the family coffers. With seven of us, two of them little shavers still at home, Mom couldn't work.

I said I earned $2 less than the actual amount I was earning every week. That gave me a enough skimmed money each week to feed my black Nibs habit, the occasional Snickers bar, and dimes to play the pinball machines at the local bowling alley, which my stepdad said was "A waste of money."

Oh, my friends were outraged. "Did you hear that Billy has to pay rent to live at home?" I didn't view it that way. I knew our family of seven could use the money.

But that Christmas I wished I had lied more, saying I was earning $5 less so each week I'd have extra money to buy myself a nice Christmas gift or two--like a new Louisville Slugger baseball bat, Ray Bradbury books, *The Martian Chronicles,* or *Dandelion Wine,* or a new rod and reel. And they would never buy me new things like that. To them, those were luxuries. Why buy new ones when the old ones--tacked-together bat, old library books, and bamboo fishing pole--did their jobs just fine?

So if I wanted any of those gifts for myself, I would have to give up my weekly heist of Nibs, Snickers, and pinball games for a dozen weeks or so. Couldn't do it.

In looking back to those growing-up years I never realized the profusion of gifts that surrounded me: fantastic friends; adoring newspaper customers, kind classmates and sports peers.

Other gifts were teachers who appreciated my love of learning; the ravine in the empty lot across the street where I dug out arrowheads and rare ancient fossils from the Pleistocene Ice Age; a night sky of such ebony blackness, filled with the gray spray of the Milky Way and stars so sharp and large I could almost reach up and grab them; nature, with the pungent prairie rose; fireflies to clap into a Ball jar to blink overnight in our bedroom; peeping and croaking frogs; meadowlarks and foxes and gophers and badgers and whitetail deer, and every day something else just as wonderful.

Many years later I wrote a piece titled "You Can Choose How You Feel," and began to realize how much of life comes down to how we choose to view its components, positively or not.

So this Christmas season I can once again tick off all the gifts that surround me, and that I often take for-granted.

Dealing With Dogs

As a kid I always loved dogs. When I was 5, I didn't realize we were struggling to get enough to eat after Mom divorced my dad and moved us to our new little town, but I would find "wild dogs," as I called them, and bring them into the house and feed them and name them.

Each time I cried when Mom said the next morning, "Old Blackie/Spot/Fido must have gotten out last night."

After Mom remarried we had other pets, but never dogs. So when I began delivering newspapers when I was 10, I figured a bonus could be playing with dogs on my route, which worked great. Except for two dogs.

The first problem dog was Tippy, a small mongrel who lived in a house on my way home. He hobbled, limping alongside his owners in their yard. Not unfriendly, but with a dark look in his eyes.

One day without his owners around, I heard him yelping and growling, but I wasn't worried because of his bad leg. Imagine my shock when he raced across the lawn and locked his jaws on the cuff of my pants leg. I kicked him off, and sped away on my bicycle.

Because I daydreamed so much, Tippy got my pants cuff several times. I finally solved it by taking a different route home.

The second dog incident happened one morning when I opened the door to a screened-in porch to toss in the doctor's newspaper and spotted a full package of butter on the floor.

Should I awaken the owners? But it was very early, and silent. Nobody was up. The doctor might have been up late tending patients. I decided to ignore it.

Then I saw the butter had been mutilated with deep jagged holes. Dog tooth marks. Big ones.

A large dog, I thought. Uh oh. I dropped the paper inside and high-tailed. Why would they gave their dog butter to eat?

A week later with my imagination roaming in dinosaur land as usual, I was oblivious to the real world. As I dropped the paper in the doctor's door, and headed toward my bike, a terrifying growl knocked me out of my reverie. Fifteen feet away in some shrubs stood a huge German Shepherd. The doctor's kids had told me in school that Brutus was harmless. I knew I was about to find out.

The hair bristled on my arms and the nape of my neck. Brutus glowered, snarling, his lips drawn back, revealing long sharp teeth. Was he out for revenge, believing I had reported his butter-biting to his masters?

I backed slowly down the sidewalk, my eyes always on Brutus, then headed out towards my bicycle on the street. As he followed me, looking to be in attack mode, I lifted the newspaper bag to protect my neck, glancing around for help, but nothing moved in the early morning silence. I wanted to scream but a fear clutched my vocal cords like a vise.

Snarling, black lips quivering, Brutus attacked me. His bared teeth gleamed in the sun. As he leaped at me, I kicked with my left foot, and smacked him squarely in his throat, feeling something soft give.

He crumpled like a sack of potatoes in the middle of the street. He lay coughing and gasping for breath, as stunned as I was. He whined, and coughed more and looked at me and then away.

I ran to my bike, peering over my shoulder. Was he following? To my relief he wasn't.

After that, every time I saw Brutus, he eyed me uncertainly, and whimpered, but never came after me again.

The doctor did not renew his newspaper subscription, so my dog problems were solved.

Just Desserts

I have always loved arrowheads, ever since unearthing pieces of worked flint in the empty lot across the street from where I grew up. During the Dirty 30s, oldsters told of walking into wind-scoured dry fields and nabbing arrowheads by the hundreds. Not my fate.

Occasionally, on a frigid winter day my newspaper customer Chissie Ackerman at the far edge of town grabbed me by the lapel of my parka as I tossed the newspaper into her door, and propelled me inside. She guided me into a chair, removed my overshoes, shoes, and socks, and rubbed circulation back into my frozen feet. As her long fingers massaged my toes, she talked about her arrowhead collection. On my lucky days she brought them out and showed them to me, how the grooves and flutes and edges had been made.

My brother and I could never find any arrowheads, so we decided to steal some. No way could we break into the Ackermans' home, but a few blocks away, on the sides of a birdbath in Arlie's yard were cemented dozens of arrowheads and spear points. To assuage our guilt a little, my brother muttered how Arlie's collection could just as well have been thrown away. "Nobody ever gets to see them. What a waste." We determined to change that.

A few days later, one evening dressed in black, we skulked through shadows, avoiding the pools of rain-streaked streetlights. At Arlie's we glanced guiltily up and down the street, and nudged apart the wet leaves of his hedge. The branched scraped ominously against our windbreakers. So began our life of crime.

What if one of the shadows, now visible on the window shade passing supper bowls back and forth, lifted the shade and glanced out? We'd be dead ducks.

"Hssst!" my brother said. "Get over here."

I knelt by the birdbath, smelling odiferous earth, feeling wetness seep into my pants and my hands. I was struck by the similarity to praying. I shuddered. If we got caught, we'd need many prayers.

But my brother hadn't been worried. "What could go wrong?" he said.

"Schotzie," I said.

"Ach, Schotzie is blind and deaf and has no teeth."

"Hsst," my brother said again. "Billy, get with it."

With Mom's kitchen knife I loosened an arrowhead. It dropped to the earth. I patted the slimy ground and found it just as Arlie's back door popped open.

I was about to leap up and run when Arlie said, "*Nuh nuh, woh gehen sie, Schotzie?*" Where are you going, Schotzie?

Followed by the clinking of dog tags as the senile beast staggered toward us. The clinking sounded like chains. Appropriate, I thought, considering our upcoming incarceration in solitary in prison.

"*Vass isht loss mit du? Nein, nein, bleib! Bleib!*" What's wrong with you? No, no, stay! Stay!

Schotzie stopped, gazing wistfully in our general direction before he whined, and turned back. "*Braver hund, Schotzie.*" Good dog, Schotzie.

Lucky for us Arlie was short-sighted, as he always said. He petted Schotzie and whispered. Schotze did his duty, flung a last longing glance in our direction, climbed the steps with effort, and followed his master into the house. I finally exhaled.

We fled with our rewards clinking in our pockets, as though chased by banshees. At home Mom gazed at me and said, "What is that all over your knees? And hands?" She stepped close, and sniffed. "*Ach du lieber.* Oh the heavens. "What have you been you doing?"

I lied, realizing the wages of sin in this case was not death, but copious dog poop.

A Christmas Thief

For a long while after my arrowhead thievery, I feared a special place might be reserved in hell for people who stole--especially during Christmas. My excuse was that I wasn't getting enough gifts--and certainly not the right ones.

Following three consecutive years of one measly gift each Christmas, socks, or underwear, or a bow tie, I decided that my folks were cheap. Mr. and Mrs. Scrooge. Some of my friends got good stuff, like toy tractors or Monopoly games they displayed in the cloakroom during recess after the holidays. Or a transistor radio for the real lucky ones.

I still lusted after a two-gun holster set so I could practice and perfect the cross-draw I'd seen in westerns on TV, left hand flashing across my body to whip out the pistol from the right holster, right hand to the left holster. Even more so because my absent father had once promised me a two-gun holster but never delivered.

Of course, I never considered why gifts from my folks might have been cheap--supporting a household of seven people on the salary of a tile mechanic/clerk, five growing boys, including a new baby. But of that concept I was oblivious. Even the bag of goodies we received at church after reciting our Bible verses on Christmas eve was more exciting: would there be chocolate in it this year? And what kind of hard candy?

Because I had been delivering *The Minneapolis Tribune* and a few *Minneapolis Star* newspapers for a year, I was pleasantly surprised to get a few gifts from my customers: homemade ammonia cookies, a silver dollar, a roll of pennies, and a stack of back issues of *Coin World* magazine, with the continuing offer of subsequent issues after they were through with the latest issue..

My regulars knew I was an ardent coin collector, because I'd spread the word liberally as I sat at their kitchen tables some evenings, chatting while they searched for money to pay for their subscription. My hidden agenda was the hope that they would hand over some of their old silver Standing Liberty coins to me. When an Indian head penny turned up in the roll of pennies, even though it was a common date, it was pretty exciting.

But that was about it. I waited for other customer's presents to appear, but the Grinch seemed to have gotten them all.

Until Sunday morning the week of Christmas, halfway across town, with my breath white and visible, I opened the outer door of a high school teacher's house to toss in the thick paper. I then checked between the outer and inner doors of all my customers in case some had left me a gift.

I was surprised to see a large green wreath hanging on the door, festooned with individually-wrapped candies, including my favorites--peppermint, butterscotch, lemon--but couldn't figure out how they'd known which ones I liked.

There was no Christmas card or note to me. I stood for a moment, breathing hard, considering: and what to my wondering mind should appear, but the realization that who else could the candy be for, if not for me? Who else came to their door, trudging or biking through the snow and frigid darkness, except me?

So I lifted the wreath. Off its hook. Stuffed it in my bag, and slogged through the rest of my route, sucking various candies as I went.

As the silent snow drifted down, enveloping me in my own private little fog as I walked, delivering the rest of my route, I felt guilty. Had I stolen the wreath?

By the time I got home I'd eaten so many of the candies that I couldn't return the wreath back and claim innocence.

A Christmas thief--I've lived with that little burden the rest of my life.

Death of a Bully

I figured the bully, George, was a goner. I was 12, and chicken to sled down Fercho hill--unlike George. I was afraid of the 45-degree grade, worse, the huge cement bulk oil tank supports at the bottom. Hit them and I'd hurt myself bad. Maybe kill myself.

Even worse, someone had used a recent snowfall to build a couple of launching ramps on the slope. They were dangerous. Sure, I could sled sedately to either side of them, but then I'd risk being branded a gutless weenie. So I needed an excuse not to sled down. I could tell the others did too.

Then I hit on it. "Damn!" I swore loudly to emphasize my disappointment. "Loose runner. Damn! Can't go down the hill!."

I waggled my hand back and forth on the runner to make it look loose. Saw a couple others wished they had thought of that.

"Use my sled," Chuck said.

My jaw dropped. Now what? But I was saved as George showed up, asking why nobody was sledding down the hill. Somebody said we'd just gotten there.

"I don't believe you chickens. Buk buk buk." He flapped his arms. "Scared of my launching pads, buk buk buk. Have to show you chickens how to be men."

He raced to the edge, and dived over the lip of the hill, landing atop his sled, and hurtled downward. At the first launching ramp he soared five feet into the air, screaming "Wahoo!" crashed down, and launched off the second ramp. Out of control.

Just then a bulk oil truck appeared on the road at the bottom of the hill. "Oh no!" we howled. Unless George could slow down, he and the truck would cross. Unless the driver saw him.

Which he didn't. George tried to skid, but he was going too fast. He slid under the moving 10-ton vehicle.

"Holy crap!" Aloys said. We screamed. George was a bully, and nobody liked him, but we didn't want to see him killed. I thought he was dead. Decapitated, or flattened. Would we see pieces of his mangled body on the road, a loose arm or leg lying about?

But the truck passed and left no bodily pieces. Was he still dragging under the truck and getting minced up? Couldn't see him.

Then Chuck said, "Look! Across the road. His sled."

It lay upended against a cement support. George sprawled in the snow nearby. He didn't move.

"He looks dead," somebody whispered.

"Uh oh," someone else said.

As I lifted my sled to head down the hill, Chuck said, "I thought your runner was too loose."

I realized I wasn't thinking about being afraid. I said, "Er, not as bad as I thought. And George needs help."

As we neared George, we saw his right arm was bent unnaturally, and his head was against the cement, bleeding.

"Is he dead?" Chuck said. "Never saw anyone dead."

I checked his pulse. "No. Still a pulse. Knocked out."

We rubbed his face with snow. Long moments later George moaned and slowly opened his eyes. He looked at us blankly. "What happened?" he gasped. "What are all you chickens doing here?"

"You got knocked out," I said. "We're checking on you."

Chuck added, "We worried you were dead."

Aloys said, "We're glad you're not."

George looked startled. His eyes filled with tears. He sat up, grimacing and clutching his broken arm. "Ouch. Must have sprained it," he said. He rubbed his tears away and said, "Wind is sure sharp."

When we offered help, he said, "I can stand." He tried, but yowled and fell.

"Let us help you," I said. "Let's get him on the sled," I said.

Aloys said he'd pull George, who had to look away and rub his eyes once more.

Even a bully had feelings. After that, George was a changed kid.

Pinch-Hitter

As a short sixth-grader watching my Wishek town amateur baseball team one summer day, the team coach yanked me from the stands, and sent up to pinch hit against players 15 to 20 years older than me. Wow! A chance to prove how good I was!

"Crouch!" the manager said, pushing me toward the batter's box. "And don't swing," he hissed.

What? The purpose of entering the batter's box is to swing, even if the pitcher is 15 years older.

The pitcher shook his head when I stepped into the batter's box. Then he wound up, and pitched. Ball one, high, ball two, low. Pitch three whizzed across the plate. I swung with all my might and missed. The manager yelped, called time, raced out and through clenched teeth said, "I said don't swing!"

I nodded sweetly. Ball three. The next pitch was a groover. I smiled and swung, watching it smack the sweet spot of the bat and soar out over the right fielder's head and the fence for a home run. At least, in my own mind. Instead, I connected with nothing but air.

The manager swore a blue streak. But what could he do? He had no one else to bat, though I did see him looking into the stands again.

Full count. I wiggled the bat. The next pitched bounced in front of the plate. Ball four. My chance at being a hero ended.

To this day, I'm not sure what that scenario was about: an injured player, I think, on a team that only had nine players. Must have been the bottom of the ninth inning too, because I didn't have to play in the field after batting. Or maybe they just played with eight?

Though my baseball talent was minimal--which I didn't yet realize--that episode fueled my dream of playing pro ball.

Catching A No-Hitter

Nine of 11 players on our high school team were left-handed, and due to physics, second, third, short, and catcher require only northpaws. Southpaws in those spots will only hurt the team. So every game we had several players not in optimal positions, which helped us build our consecutive-loss string to about 40.

Which didn't really weigh on me, because I loved to play the game. Baseball was in my blood.

While playing third base in high school ball I never threw out a single batter, because unlike righties, after fielding I had to turn my body to throw (the physics part), which allowed the racing batter extra steps to first base before my throw got there.

Playing catcher as a left-hander was most frustrating of all, but also my greatest claim to baseball fame: I caught a no-hitter.

Doug Kramer was pitching, all elbows, knees, wild eyes, and wilder pitches with absolutely zero control of what I suspect was an 80-plus mph blazing heater. I was catching.

I was petrified of his high-speed fastball. Each one smacked into my catcher's mitt, burning my palm until a constant flame settled there. So I flinched. Sometimes closed my eyes just as he pitched. Had a ton of passed balls. Couldn't throw anybody out, so the Linton players who got on base--many through errors and walks had a heyday, stealing second and third, scurrying around the bases, scoring on wild pitches, walks or errors. A couple of balks.

Doug walked 12 and threw 10 wild pitches, and I made about 10 errors as catcher trying to grab his speedy offerings, while our team contributed at least half a dozen errors.

We lost, 27-2. But it didn't matter. Other than my throbbing hand, I was in my glory, playing baseball, one step from my dream of a career as a New York Yankee.

Many years later on the phone, the first words from my high school friend Doug were, "Do you remember the game where I smacked that liner over that Becker kid from Napoleon at second in the bottom of the ninth driving you in from second base with the winning run?"

Doug got right to the point, even if it occurred decades ago.

Of course I remember the game. I'm reminded of it every year as professional baseball playoffs loom, because that was our only playoff game ever. And the only high school baseball game we ever won in four years. But we had that left handed physics excuse.

Ervin Attends the Movies

I had never seen the Dakota Theatre movie projectors until one day as a ninth-grader when Walter Sayler, the owner, asked if I'd like to make extra money running the projectors, one of the many ways people of our little town watched out for us.

The first time I climbed the stairs and stepped into the projection room with its giant steel door and thick cement walls, I was overwhelmed, stunned by the size of the machines.

I would be operating these monsters, taller than me? Impossible! And immediately I was brought up short being warned of the dangers: with a jaunt into carelessness I could get electrocuted; or momentarily light-blinded; or crack the reflecting mirror costing thousands; or burn the film; screw up the sound; insert the wrong reel and goof up the movie for a hundred restless natives below.

The booth contained two identical giant Simplex Peerless movie projectors, seven feet high with upper and lower reel containers. The round fat main body had brilliant arc rod lighting.

As projectionist at the Dakota Theatre in Wishek, I ran a Peerless Simplex movie camera like this one.

On the plus side, being paid to be in charge of such expensive, dangerous, and complicated machinery increased my self-confidence. I felt like an adult. I was being trusted. Plus I could watch the movies free. And "be paid" while doing homework, or reading books by Ray Bradbury.

I started working as projectionist, running shows like "Last Train From Boot Hill," "Spartacus," "The Ten Commandments," and lesser ones like "Zotz," which required handing out plastic tokens that said "Zotz."

As a perk, before and after movies I could stand in the lobby greeting people, and glow in their comments about my basketball skills in games we'd played that week.

Each movie was five or six 2,000-foot rolls of 35mm film on a 20-inch metal reel, 22 minutes, weighing 15 pounds.

Each Thursday evening I fast-forwarded through the reels to detect tears, and repair them, and spliced the cartoon and previews together.

One time I brought my friend, Ervin, up to the projectionist room on a movie night. Ervin was 24 years older, his brain frozen at age 13 when he fell off a hay rack and cracked his skull on the edge.

Ervin stepped into the high-ceilinged-booth as into a cathedral, his eyes huge as they rested on the pair of seven-foot-high projectors. "That's what makes the movie," I said.

"But but but Biddee!" he said. "They're so big! So big!" He gazed at me with awe. "You do this all alone?"

I nodded. "Like you when you run a tractor or combine."

He gaped when I pulled out a reel of film from its metal box. "So big!" He said.

I loaded the film and started it to show him how it worked. Agape, Ervin stared out as the movie scrolled onto the screen. I showed him how everything worked. "Ooh, Biddy," was all he said, wringing his hands.

At movie time, the arc rods buzzed as I lit them, started the film to ramp it up, waited eight seconds, opened the dowser, and activated the sound. The arc light reflected off the large concave mirror, through the film and lens onto the giant screen. Like a miracle, Daffy Duck and Porky Pig performed their shenanigans.

With two minutes left, a bell warned me to prepare for the changeover to the next reel in the other machine. With eight seconds remaining a round cue appeared in the upper right corner of the screen, the signal to start the second machine, which I had loaded earlier. Seven seconds later a second cue allowed me one second to switch over. Done right, the movie was seamless.

I felt privileged, and loved being a movie projectionist. Even did it in my college town.

Twenty years later, my brother Ron attended a movie at Dakota Theatre. He waved at Ervin and sat down. During the show, the projectionist missed a switchover. Film flapped and the screen went white. Ervin glared up at the projectionist' booth and yelled, "Heyyy! When Biddee Vossler was projectionist, stuff like that never happened!"

Ervin the stalwart. Loyal to the end. Another gift in my fortunate life.

I was a projectionist at this Dakota Theatre, starting when I was a ninth grader, running shows Friday, Saturday, and Sunday nights.

A Developing Miracle

During my sophomore year I fell in love with photography when a teacher at his house showed me images he'd just developed. Black and white, of course.

"You'll really like this, Billy," he said, leading me into a dark room with a red light. He closed the door. The scene turned eerie, seemingly light and dark at the same time.

As he used the enlarger to expose a piece of shiny Kodak paper with light shone on it for a short time through a piece of film, he explained the process. He slid the paper into a tray of developing fluid, and swished it around with a tongs.

"Now comes the miracle," he said, softly.

Black marks began to appear on the paper, getting darker and darker with each swish until a photo of several people appeared.

"Whoa!" I said. "That is a miracle!"

After a couple more, he let me create a photo. As my picture appeared, I thought, another miracle! I shivered. And was hooked.

Thus began my photography passion. With an old camera I started shooting photos. But had to cut way back when I discovered how expensive printing each roll was at the drugstore.

Then I realized I could develop the film and print the photos by myself, just as he was doing. And much cheaper. And have great and miraculous fun, from that one experience with the teacher, who unfortunately moved away at the end of the year.

No one in town sold photographic chemicals, so I had to wait until our band traveled to Jamestown for the State Music Contest. I sneaked away to a camera shop that sold what I needed.

The next problem was creating a dark room. Where in our house would work? Somewhere in the basement seemed obvious.

Except I couldn't adhere anything to the concrete wall to cover the windows.

The last resort was our double bed. That is, beneath it. I draped heavy covers over the sides, and crawled under for a test. Ten minutes later, the pitch black darkness remained.

With a red light bulb amidst a few stray dust bunnies I'd missed, I set up the photography materials I'd bought: a Patterson developing tank and reels for film, trays, Kodak professional photo developer, fixer, and stop bath, and a flashlight.

Because I couldn't afford an enlarger, I used a big magnifying glass, with spotty results--mostly unfocused pictures. So I realized if I really wanted to develop good photos, I needed an enlarger.

To make extra money to buy more photo equipment, over and above what I earned delivering papers, I sold candles, photo scrapbooks, stationery, and fountain pens mostly to my customers until I had enough money for an enlarger.

By pure luck, our superintendent of schools took his son and me to a movie in Jamestown one day, which allowed me to buy my enlarger. Now I was in business.

From the top of our house I took dozens of pictures from all directions, and while playing baseball, and shooting baskets, and numerous ones of our pet rabbit Oliver, suspended in mid-air with his legs splayed after I flung him up, and my brother caught him. And developed and printed the photos under the bed, still in awe at the miracle each time a photo appeared on Kodak paper.

As I look back, I wish I had taken many more pictures, of the swimming pool, park, WPA work, depot, elevators, the empty lot, Wishek in general, recording how the town looked in those days. But I didn't; and unfortunately, only a few early pix remain today.

What does remain, however, is a love of photography that increased my proficiency, and helped me create photos acceptable to magazines, which bought my articles. The skill allowed me to print all the photos in five of my books.

Funny how things work out. Though photography started as a hobby, my love of it has morphed into a central, fun and useful, part of my life.

To see my photos, check out my Bill Vossler FaceBook site, where I add four new pictures each day, about nature, animals, travels, and much more.

The first photo I developed under our basement bed "darkroom."

Undesirable Nickname

Of the nicknames I accumulated growing up, the most troubling was "Overshoes." I'd begun delivering newspapers wearing hand-me-down shoes that developed flopping soles, made workable by rubber bands or string wrapped around the toes.

Winter snows got my feet cold and wet, requiring repeated trips to our shoemaker, Jacob Rattei to repair. His shop smelled like new leather. He charged us a pittance each time.

But finally he said a pair of disasters could only be saved for so long, and I should tell my mother to buy me overshoes, so we could cut down on repairs.

Thus in seventh grade I got insulated overshoes big as ore boats. Along followed the nickname Overshoes. "Hey, Overshoes." "Gosh, look at the galoshes." "Are those boots or boats?"

The class bully, Jerry, especially loved to provoke me. "Hey, Vossler, I bet your real last name is Overshoes," he'd say, sneering and cursing. We were all afraid of him, relieved when he turned his attention to a single prey, but this time it happened to be me. I began to feel diminished, and worthless.

One spring day before phy ed class when I bent over to lace my tennies, Jerry kneed me in the butt and I went over on my head. I jumped up full of fire. "You big piece of crap," I said, calling him a few dirty swear words, "What's wrong with you, anyway?"

My friends laughed nervously. His face got red. The teacher was looking in our direction, and hadn't heard my outburst. So what could Jerry do? Nothing. I felt great.

He glanced at the teacher and fixed me with a murderous glare. On the way to the gym floor for dodge ball he whispered, "If I don't kill you in kisser-crusher, I'll do it after school." He made a zipping sound and sliced his hand across his neck.

Whoops! I'd been so angry, I hadn't considered the consequences.

I was distracted the rest of the day, thinking of the doom I was about to suffer at the hands--or fists--of Jerry. He'd beat up other kids, so I knew what was in store for me. He was big and strong and mean, and a veteran fighter. I was a timid twerp who had never been in a fight. I decided running for my life was the only solution.

The second the lyceum in the gym ended at the end of that school day, I launched myself off the bleachers and clomped across the gym floor in my overshoes at full speed, fleeing for survival.

But wearing big overshoes, he caught up with me halfway across the schoolyard. "Hey chicken," he said, flapping his arms, "Buk buk buk. Not so brave now, are you, without the teacher to protect you?" he said, cursing. He stepped close and raised his fist.

Somehow my fist shot out and cracked him solidly on the jaw. I gloried in hearing his teeth click together. He went down, his mouth open in surprise.

He leaped up and came at me fast. But I was emboldened. And ready. What else could I do? I lashed out again, nailing him on the chin once more. He went down again.

He licked his lips and his eyes widened at the taste of blood. I hoped he wouldn't try again, because my knuckles felt broken.

From the ground he stared at me in surprise, touching his fingers to the blood and examining it. He muttered something, but didn't move. I turned and walked away.

Obviously he had not expected me to put up a fight. I realized later that my saving grace was probably my left-handedness. He hadn't expected punches from the left side.

That ended it. He never sneered "Overshoes" at me again.

Paper Route Monopoly

By my junior year in high school, my brother and I had locked down a monopoly on delivering newspapers in my town of 1,288 Germans from Ukraine. We delivered two dailies--*The Minneapolis Tribune,* and *The Minneapolis Star,* while *Grit* was monthly.

From delivering newspapers I learned how to deal with people, paying the bills to the paper company on time, doing my job in wind, rain, or bitter cold. But I discovered other things too.

For instance, that my mother shaded the truth. She'd cry, "*Steig oof",* Wake up, to us in our basement bed. "It's almost 6:30."

In those days kids didn't get an alarm clock in their room. When I came upstairs to her call, the clock always showed much earlier--6:05 to 6:15. "Almost 6:30" was a good 20 minutes away.

When I complained she said, "You're up, aren't you?"

I had to be diligent, to deliver every paper to every customer every day. If I missed one, I had to replace it and, in the process skip breakfast or be tardy to school, or worse yet, come late to baseball or basketball practice. Newspapers were of prime importance and taken very seriously, and customers watched for them. When I got home from my route, if there was a paper which hadn't been delivered--a huge rarity of maybe twice in 9 years--I'd hear about it.

So I divided my route into natural groups of streets. If I had six papers between our house and the EUB church, I pulled six papers out of my bag, and delivered them. If I had an extra when the next group of customers was to start, I could quickly figure out who I'd missed, and backtrack. Then I pulled out the eight papers for customers from the church to the swimming pool. And so on.

I also depended on my English teacher's dog, Iff, so-named because of his bark. Mr. Erickson lived across the street from us so

Iff shadowed me almost every day. He knew my route. If I was daydreaming or inventing stories or just glorying in nature, and threatened to miss a customer, he alerted me by running across that lawn or heading to their door to remind me.

I also learned how to handle money. To complete the newspaper monopoly, I worked at the *Wishek Star*, our local weekly newspaper when I was 12, sweeping floors, carrying out trash, watching how everybody worked. I learned how newspapers were made, an entirely different process than today.

I loved watching Muff type away at the Linotype machine keyboard, and feeling the high heat of the liquid lead that cooled into slugs long as a credit card, half as wide, and three times as thick. On top of each edge were raised, backwards-written words. Each finished slug clicked into place, adding one more line of writing in a column that helped make up a page in the *Wishek Star*. When he'd finished the correct number of pages, they were inked, and thousands of copies run. So much to learn! So much fun!

Because of all those early risings (Thanks, Mom!) and hours and miles of deliveries, I received an amazing gift, familiarizing me with words, how to put sentences together, all of which led to my life's work as a writer.

Meeting American Indians

Growing up in a small town with the vast majority who were white Germans-from-the Ukraine, I had no experience with American Indians--except for Tonto in "The Lone Ranger," and warriors in western movies who seemed to lose every battle. Until one day while digging up tiny white bones unearthed by a gopher in the empty lot across the street from our house.

I was 10. My eyes grew big when an inch-long deadly-looking arrowhead appeared. I marveled at the edges, still sharp after hundreds of years. Digging furiously I thunked into a solid surface, a rock half the size of a loaf of bread. I cleared off dirt crumbles, revealing a smooth grooved channel around its center, where doubtless a rawhide thong had secured it to a handle.

I trembled with excitement. A war club!

I froze when I saw dried red blood on the business end. Unschooled as I was in artifacts, I didn't realize it could not be dried blood. But that's what I believed, and I was elated.

I turned the club over and over, rubbing the blood, thinking about a warrior hundreds of years ago--thousands?--who had lain in wait on this very spot for his prey.

But what prey? Rabbit? Gopher? Fox? Deer? Human? I tried to imagine what he looked like, but couldn't get much past Tonto.

My first real contact with live American Indians came playing basketball my junior year in high school. Which is the first part of the story.

During the dead of winter the Fort Yates Warriors from the Standing Rock Sioux Indian Reservation came to my home town for a game. Ranked No. 1 in Class B in the state, our gym was packed.

We shot pre-game lay-ups while the crowd rustled and murmured. Then the door to the visitor locker room burst open.

Out surged a dozen American Indian boys dressed in full-length gold warm-ups with blue trim. Our home crowd was stunned into silence--by the unfamiliar beauty of their copper skins and jet-black hair, by the smooth grace of their gliding bodies as they circled the gymnasium, poetry in motion. The only sounds were the squeaks of their tennis shoes on the wood floor as they rounded the corners.

Their surprising display must have unsettled us. Halfway through the first quarter we were down 10-0. But we chipped away, took the lead with about two minutes left in the game, and won by four points.

A couple of months later at the regional tournament in Dickinson, we faced the Fort Yates Warriors again, this time with the opportunity to go to the state tournament on the line if we won this game, and the next. With five seconds to go, we led by two, but they had the ball. We could almost taste the state tournament!

The clock ticked down--four, three, two! Morris Elk Nation had the ball, and was guarded heavily. He faked, shot, was fouled. The ball banked off the backboard and through the rim, tying the score. The buzzer sounded. He calmly buried the free throw. Ecstasy for us turned into agony. No state tournament for us.

An hour later, crushed and numb, we all retreated into a room of our motel, studies in despondency, lamenting this tragedy of epic proportions that we were sure we would never ever overcome.

Suddenly there was a sharp rap on the door. Who could that be? Somebody opened the door, and there stood most of the Fort Yates team--bearing boxes of pizza.

"You guys must be hungry," Elk Nation said.

They crowded in until we were elbow-to-elbow, munching away, chatting about plays we'd made. One warrior said, "I didn't want the game to end, it was so much fun playing against you guys." Another said, "You're the best team we played all year."

"But clean," another added softly, his eyes distant.

Finally the boxes were empty. They rose and filed out, waving shyly. Last was Morris Elk Nation. At the door he turned and said, "We hated to beat you."

Then he was gone, my brush with real warriors.

The Joys of Ice Fishing

One Saturday when I was a teen during the deep cold of North Dakota winter, three friends and I piled into Doug's '56 Studebaker, and cruised the roller coaster hills south of Wishek on our way to Green Lake to ice fish.

Over the last rise, and the final curve, and there the lake stretched out like the broad gray back of the ocean. A frozen ocean.

Cold penetrated the fish house, the ceiling, the walls, the floor, our gloves, the soles of our boots. We fired the kindling and the stove fought against the chill. By the time we skimmed the ice from the holes in the corners, baited the hooks, set out the filleting board, pans and butter, and sorted out the playing cards, the little shack was heated up. We were even sweating--and like adolescents everywhere, constantly hungry.

In the clear water we saw fish swim slowly by, their tails stroking--a few northern pike, but mostly perch. We dropped our lines through the holes in the ice, and while we waited for meals to attach themselves to the ends of our hooks, we played cards. "Deal them suckers!" someone would bellow.

Sometime during the hooting and hollering and slapping down of aces and kings a bobber would tremble, jerk, and disappear. Cards would fly and so would the owner of the bobber. "Take the bait hard, you little beast," he might whisper solemnly as he fingered the line.

Then the perch ran, and cards were forgotten as we yanked up the squirming wriggling fish, unhooking them as fast as we could and tossing them out the fish house door, flipping and flopping, onto the ice, while a huge cloud of vapor drifted in each time.

We filleted enough for a meal, brushed them with plenteous butter, or rolled the fillets in cracker crumbs and egg dip, and sizzled them in the frying pan on the stove. The aroma was a slice of heaven, buoyed by the smell of grandma's homemade bread.

As we hunched over the small table shoveling in the perch and bread and milk, I glanced at my trio of fishing mates one by one, Doug, Tom, and Vern, and tears sprang into my eyes. I was grateful for the muted flickering light of the candles, for how could I have explained how overcome I was by the depth of my love for these comrades?

By fate we had been dropped into this small town at the same time, bonding in school, sometimes through work hauling bales or picking rock together, running around with the same girls as friends, playing tennis or pool or basketball, and yet, here we were, fishing together, bantering, still enjoying each other's company. A lump rose in my throat. How could I have been so lucky?

Hours later we gathered our gear, the fish we hadn't eaten, and stepped out into the utter blackness. If chasms had existed in the ice outside the door we would have fallen through them, and the frigid waters of Green Lake would have swallowed us.

I gazed with astonishment up at the diamonds of stars, seemingly close enough to grab a handful and yank them out of the sky and slide them into my pocket.

Then the ice began to crack--crrrr-uuuu-ccc--kkk, the earth breathing and the beauty of it all, the glory, the nature, the stars, the friendships swelled my heart to overflowing.

The others were impatient to get going. If we didn't get back in time, our high school would not have a basketball game that night. All four of us were starters on the team.

The breeze was fire against my cheeks, but I stood there, amazed at the grandeur of my life at that moment, and I wanted to continue feeling it, until Doug revved the car as a reminder.

I'm glad I dallied on the ice that day, reliving all that love. Those were some of the most powerful male friendships of my life, and that intensity has rarely returned.

Buck Fever

Yeah yeah yeah, I thought, trying to shut out the old-timer's words as we trudged through the brush. He was a talker, a white current of words spewing from his mouth into the cold fall air. My eyes kept darting around, hoping to spot a big whitetail buck and bring him down with one quick shot of my borrowed 30.06; that would shut the old guy up.

At 19, this was my first deer hunt. This older experienced member of the party rambled on in a low voice, "Watch out for buck fever."

Every deer hunter knew about the dreaded buck fever, when the hunter froze or trembled so violently the sight of the magnificent target that they couldn't get off an accurate shot.

I tried not to listen, but still caught snatches of words. "...best hunters...my first time...trembling hands...adjust...aim just in front." *Yeah yeah yeah*, I thought. I'd hunted gophers and blackbirds and foxes and badgers. How difficult could it be to hunt something that much bigger?

The brush grabbed our legs until we stopped at a choice spot on the slant of a hill rising above a depression filled with reeds and puffy cattails in water. A bare brown verge would funnel the deer right to whoever was lucky enough to sit here on the brittle grass. Who, to my surprise they said, would be me.

"Sit there," he said. I sat a few feet away. "Canadian thistle," I said, pointing.

He smiled. He'd known it. "Be alert. It'll happen fast." *Yeah yeah yeah*. He shook his rifle and grinned. "Don't let buck fever get you!" *Yeah yeah yeah*. They all moved off.

A while later I heard crashing in the brush atop the rise 200 feet away. I assumed he was returning to offer me additional unwanted advice. I was daydreaming about a particular black-haired girl when a dark shape hove into my peripheral vision.

The buck stood at the lip of the hill, surveying his domain. He lifted his snout and sniffed the air. I was downwind so he couldn't smell me. He glanced over his shoulder, and trotted down the slope toward me. I drew in my breath sharply. A gorgeous eight-point buck with black-rimmed whitish ears, black snout, brown and reddish body and restless liquid black eyes, which fixed on me, an alien object in his landscape, then moved away. Tendrils of white smoke jetted out from his nostrils, and his flank was wet.

He glanced back over his shoulder. I heard a faint sound behind him. When his eyes looked the other way, I raised the rifle and put the stock against my shoulder. He turned back, and moved toward me and to my shock, stopped 15 feet away, below me, breathing hard, a full side view, as though posing. I'd never seen a deer so close. I could have spit on him. He was a glorious sight. My being was overcome with his living beauty.

How could I miss? He was the size of a railroad boxcar. He stood with immense dignity, white breath feathering out, a gorgeous beast, a shareholder with me on this earth. His eyes settled on me. I shivered.

"You'll be shooting downward. Aim high." Or was it low? My heart hammered in my throat. I was astonished to see my rifle tremble. Buck fever!

I'd been holding my breath. I had to exhale or burst. I aimed at his shoulder, and pulled the trigger. The rifle leaped.

So did the buck. The bullet pricked the hill on the far side of the slough. His sinews bunched and drove him up the hill and away at astonishing speed, his hooves clattering on pebbles. Then he was gone.

Sighing, I lowered my rifle. Happiness flooded my heart. Lucky I never was good at listening to unsolicited advice.

The Wall

The itinerant who changed my life drifted into town one cool spring evening before I turned 17. My friends and I were sitting in Weintz Café about 8 PM, ruing the end of basketball season.

We were sipping chocolate malts when the door clattered open and a wizened little man entered. He had sharp features, sharper eyes and a fading mustache. And radiated a sense of joy.

He set down two five-gallon pails, surveyed the long wall opposite us, and grinned. I looked; all I could see was a wall of no great distinction.

He shook out a tarp across three booths, opened a can of paint, stepped up onto the cloth on the seat of the booth, and streaked green on the wall. Alarmed, I looked at Mrs. Weintz. She glanced at him, then went into the kitchen.

With a folding ruler he traced pencil marks on the wall. He tore off five-foot strips of masking tape, placing one vertically at each end, 30 feet apart.

With our malts finished, Tom and Doug wanted to drag main. I shook my head. "I want to see what he does."

Just then he said, "You guys want to help with this mural?"

"Mural?" Doug said.

"What kind of help?" I asked.

"The tape," he said, holding up a roll. "The animals."

"Animals?" we said. "What animals?" He had our attention. We all loved nature and animals.

He held up the rolls. "Tape first, animals later. Careful now. Eyes will migrate to a crooked border instead of to the beauty of the scene. The animals." He smiled, and the room brightened.

As he worked, he said painting murals provided a change of pace from his main job of writing magazine articles.

My jaw dropped. Writing as a job? "I didn't know you could make a living writing."

He smiled. "You can't. At least not a good living." He raised the paint brush. "Which is why I paint. Among other things."

I said I'd always dreamed about being a writer.

"Dreams are good," he said. "Life's beacons. They light up the way to go." He smiled. "Now excuse me. Time to paint."

Fine with me. I was overwhelmed with thoughts of being a writer. Make a living--at writing? What could be more fun?

My head whirled. Hemingway and Steinbeck were writing giants. An average person could become a writer?

His sure hand stroked a sky and a mountain range onto the wall. The smell of fresh paint filled the silent room. He pointed a brush at us. "So, what would you like to see in this mural?"

Whatever we asked, he painted: a river, waterfall, jumping salmon. A forest, birch trees, lightning. Finally he sighed. "Enough for tonight. Let's eat!"

Tom and Doug begged off, and left, which pleased me, so the itinerant and I could talk about writing. He told me about the basics of writing, about querying, about *The Writer* and *Writer's Digest* magazines, about the joy of seeing your name in print.

Later in bed I tossed and turned, writerhood on my mind.

The next evening he painted the sun, huge thunderheads, white swirls of clouds, valleys, grasslands. Each time he smiled. "So, what kind of animals do you want here? And here? And here?" He created V's of geese, eagles circling mountain crags, seagulls, killdeer, moose, elk, deer, antelope, gophers--a veritable Noah's ark.

Afterwards we talked about writing again. When he was finished eating, I sadly watched him pack up. He held out his hand.

He saw the stricken look on my face. He smiled and patted my shoulder. "You'll be all right," he said. "You have a dream." He pointed at the wall. "Your job is to fill your world with all the color and imagination that you can muster--with words. And you will."

And then he was gone.

I still don't know who he was. I only wish I could find him to shake his hand once more and look him in the eye and say, "Thank you."

An Unusual Christmas Gift

Fifty-one years ago this Christmas season I was given the most useful critique of my life. I was attending college at Valley City (North Dakota) State College, knowing I wanted to do two things in life: teach school until I proved myself with words, and write.

But I wasn't satisfied with my choices of majors, math and chemistry. Most students didn't like math courses taught at 8 AM, too early for an active stay-up-late college kid. I'd delivered newspapers early in the morning from age 10 until attending college, so that wasn't my problem. Quadratic equations were. I wasn't learning, and I was bored. Which was why I whined.

And chemistry. I was playing Junior Varsity basketball, and chemistry labs often went far into the afternoon and interfered with practice. I didn't look forward to telling Mr. Grooters that I had a lab, and would be missing practice. Again. Besides, I could never get my organic chemistry experiments to come out right. I was floundering. And whining about my problems.

I lived on third floor of Mythaler Hall, the men's dorm, the first room as you came up the stairs. (No elevators in those days.) Our door was always open, usually with popular music playing from my stereo, so kids were always dropping in. We'd sit on the edge of the beds and chew the fat, as they say.

Just before Christmas in my sophomore year, we were doing our usual rapping and talking and singing and changing records, and as it got later and later, one by one my friends left. Except for one. He knew my roommate had to go for a smoke, or to the bathroom, and I think that's what he was waiting for. Once he and I were alone, he listened to me whine about something. Didn't matter what.

So my friend let me have my say, and then got up, and walked to the door, looking back and forth in the hallway. He turned back to me and said, "Vossler, you're the worst whiner I've ever heard in the world." And he left. And I sat there, stunned.

Christmas vacation came soon. I was absorbed in thinking about what he'd said, because I knew whining wasn't a good trait. I was quiet on my ride home, and thoughtful during my Christmas break. And eventually I came to the realization that what he'd said was true. I was a whiner.

And from that moment on, I decided to make a huge life change. I decided to quit whining, because I saw how my family members whined, and how that released a little anxiety so you didn't actually have to do anything. I discovered if I didn't whine, it meant I was going to try to do some of the things I was usually afraid of.

So from that moment on, I've worked on becoming a more positive person. That was the best gift I've ever received in my life.

How To Enjoy A Blizzard

None of central Minnesota's blizzards, though difficult, have compared to the Great Blizzard of 1966, which ended with snowdrifts 30 feet high on the prairies of North Dakota, where the only resistance to the storm was strands of barbed wire.

On March 2, 1966, after a few snowflakes drifted down into the bare trees on the steep hill behind my college dorm, the howling wind rose to 70 to 100 mph, and created a solid gray sheet of snow that obliterated the hill, piling up massive drifts. By evening the snow was piled halfway up the windows on first floor. Classes at Valley City were canceled, and still the thick snow came down.

On third floor we were a close gang of playful inmates, back for our second year on this dorm floor. We played pinochle, penny-ante poker, whist, chess, checkers, listened to music and talked smart. But at the blizzard went on, those activities paled, so we invented games, like Ban-ball: knocking over a Ban deodorant can on the floor from a distance with a tennis ball. In our underwear we luged down the wet hall on our butts. We designed variations of ping-pong in the activity center (two tables end to end, or one table side against the wall, or each player had to spin 180 degrees after each stroke), played wiffle ball with textbook bats (the psych book worked best) and other goofy games.

By the third evening, we needed a new jolt of excitement. I became the unwitting linchpin, when I wondered aloud how deep the snow had risen behind the dorm. We couldn't gauge the depth through my frosted-up window on third floor. Needed a better look.

"The bathroom," I said. "I don't think it has a screen."

In the bathroom, I unlocked the latch and grunted to pull up the window. Snow streamed in unimpeded on the screaming wings of the wild storm.

A couple of us leaned out, blinking back tears in the fierce wind, peering through the dimness. "What do you think?" I said. "Five feet?"

"I know how to find out," someone said.

We yelled encouragement as he slid through the opening and pushed off, plunging down shoes first perhaps a dozen feet, drilling deep into the snow bank up past his waist. After a few seconds others followed, and minutes later skidded back, snow-covered, into the bathroom in paroxysms of laughter. New fun!

Eventually someone offered a quarter to whoever would jump out without pants. That naturally led to an obvious end, when "Calvin" asked how much we'd pay if he went out naked.

After a moment of cheering, then consultation, we anted up 85 cents ($6.10 today--a lot of money then to a college kid).

He dropped his pants and drawers, skinned off his shirt, and while we hooted and hollered, crawled onto the sill, screamed like Tarzan, and jumped. We laughed uproariously, jostling each other for a glimpse of Calvin, a porcelain doll buried up to his armpits, freezing in the snow bank.

Calvin's roomie held open the first-floor door, and he raced up into a hot running shower. That provided a fitting end to our festivities during the worst blizzard, hands down, that I've been involved in.

Or should I say, "Pants down?"

Plowing Up Trouble

I was, I suppose, something of a danger. But I didn't mean to be. To myself or anybody else.

Growing up in a small North Dakota agricultural town--surrounded by pastures of bawling cows, waving fields of wheat like a golden ocean, farm yards filled with squawking chickens and oinking pigs, it was inevitable that I would work on farms.

The work was often backbreaking, like picking rocks which had seeped up from the deeps of the fields each spring, grabbing them and racing after the quickly-moving tractor and wagon and lobbing them in with a clunk, and bending for more, and racing and clunking--a dirty, awful job that I despised.

Or hauling up to 100-pound rectangular hay bales at three cents each, split among the number of workers. Haul 800, a really good day, $24 split three ways.

Not much danger there, except scratches on the knees or bottoms of the wrists, and getting dusty, sneezy, itchy, hot.

The timbre of danger changed when I was hired to plow a field, a boring and repetitive job while being cooped up in a silent tractor cab. Some excitement occurred occasionally when a plowshare clanged against a deep-hidden rock and jerked the tractor, the plow leaping out of the ground to protect the share.

I loved to read, so after one boring session of plowing, the next day I brought along Ray Bradbury's *Twice Twenty-Two*, a book of 44 exciting short stories by my favorite author.

With everything ready, I slid the tractor into gear, took off, and glanced behind as I lowered the plow and watched the shares slide into the dirt. I turned and checked the unplowed distance that lay ahead of me, figuring I could alternate reading for a minute, checking the plow, assessing the distance, and repeating, until I hit the end of the long field with the fence line in front of me, forcing me to turn around. At a bit more than idling speed, the tractor followed the furrow easily, so I really didn't need to steer.

I laid the open book on the steering wheel, and began reading "A Sound of Thunder," the story of a man taken back millions of years into the Cretaceous period to hunt a *Tyrannosaurus rex*, which was going to die anyway momentarily.

The story mesmerized me, Eckels following his guide on a hovering metal path he must not leave because if he stepped off and killed anything besides the *Tyrannosaurus rex*, history all the way down the line to the present could be altered. But when he spotted the live *Tyrannosaurus rex*, he spooked and fled--off the path.

Excitedly I turned the page for the climax and was brought out of my reverie by the thump of the plow striking a rock, and being thrown forward into the windshield, banging my head, while a *whang whang* sound propelled something past the window.

But the sound had come from the front of the tractor. I rubbed my head and put the tractor into neutral and glanced out the windshield and spotted what I'd done--uh oh, knocked down a series of fence poles and snapped three strands of barbed wire.

I leaped out, sweating, examining the carnage, and pondered how I might repair the damage without anybody knowing. The poles, possibly yes. Stretching the wires tight, impossible.

My boss was not pleased. "A book again, I suppose," he said, shaking his head. He added something about me being a danger, to myself and to his machinery. While swathing earlier, a board in the reel had broken. Not my fault. Really.

However, he evidently didn't hold a grudge. Later that fall he hired me to drive grain truck out into the field while he spun the John Deere combine through the wheat.

He never said I couldn't bring my books along. But that's another story.

Hay, the Time Machine

Except for the back-breaking drudgery, I loved the trappings of hauling hay bales. The uniform garnered respect, long-sleeved shirt and jeans, patched knees, work gloves, boots, and baseball cap.

Walk into the Weintz Cafe or Herr Bros. Mercantile wearing those clothes and the denizens would say, "Hauling bales, yah?" They'd smile and nod and a new light would shine in their eyes. You were a good German from the Ukraine; you knew how to work.

I loved the camaraderie borne of hard work and a shared goal, even when a friend's frailty meant double work. Jon could barely roll slough-grass bales across the field, much less heft them. So we helped him.

Friendships were forged in the fire of nature, like the time we loaded the final bales from a field, ignoring the gathering sweep of black clouds, rising wind pregnant with the smell of rain, zigzagging lightning followed by bone-crackling thunder.

The hail struck halfway to the farm. Soon I was piloting the tractor blind, shielding my eyes with one hand, while the wind howled. I would have stopped at that point, but just then we crossed the lip of a steep hill and plunged downward. I panicked and shoved in the clutch. With not enough driving time on a tractor, that was definitely the wrong thing to do.

With the tractor not slowed by being in gear, we immediately picked up terrifying speed. The landscape blurred as we rocketed downward. Bales were ejected like three-foot-long spring-loaded golden packages. I jammed on the brake. We began sliding off the road. Jon and Tom cursed as they hung onto the bucking rack.

I released the clutch once more. The tractor's rear wheels locked. The engine roared menacingly. The front end of the tractor leaped upward.

The trailer jackknifed, sliding into the rear tires of the tractor. The skidding trailer spit up clots of earth, threatening to overturn us. I screamed, "Hang on," jammed in the clutch again, and rode the raging beast, Pecos-Bill style, full speed downward.

Finally under control and on a flat area, the trailer half-empty, white bolts of lightning sizzled about my ears (as well as the epithets of my compatriots). I stopped and we jumped off while thunder boomed, and the air smelled of ozone. Bedraggled, we crawled under the trailer bed while hail clunked off the rack and clattered off the tractor.

We got paid by the bale, so having to re-handle those bales negated our day's profit. But we were alive.

I loved the finiteness of hauling bales: three cents each (later four) divided by the number of workers. After every rack, I knew exactly how rich I'd become.

The number of bales was also finite, growing smaller and smaller as the hay rack ate up the rows. When the rows were barren, and the racks empty, the job was finished.

The food was wonderful, the table groaning under platters of fried chicken, mashed potatoes, corn, tureens of gravy, pitchers of Kool-aid and milk, and sideboards packed with aromatic *kuchen* or apple pie. A feast for kings.

Nature's freshness appealed to me, smelling the fecund land, watching the thunderclouds building, studying the animals.

I have no desire to return to those days. Instead, nowadays if I want to relive my youth, I drift out to the hay lands, open the car window, inhale, and set the dial on my own personal time machine, whirling myself back into the aromatic past.

Greenhorn No More

When my buddy Frank invited me to play basketball with his hometown amateur team, coached by his brother Connie, I was elated. Every weekend during the season I went to the Redlin farm, helped with some normal farm chores--dropping bales for the cows, checking water, hauling manure, putting out salt blocks. Nothing unusual or difficult.

Last on my to-do list on a college weekend would have been going to his place to brand cattle, but I figured I could help him and Connie out. Plus it was something different.

Connie met us at the ranch, laughing, and looking at Frank, said, "Ready for a good time this weekend, Billy Boy?"

Frank coughed, saying, "We might work a few small calves." He held his palm low to the ground, indicating their sizes.

"Shouldn't be too hard. Or take too long." But he wouldn't look me in the eye.

The next morning, the roan saddled for me pegged me as a greenhorn. She dawdled along eating grass or stopped to admire the view, no matter how much I swore and urged her with my spurless heels. I could see Frank, Connie and their sister-in-law LuAnn were beginning to question the wisdom of bringing along a greenhorn.

At the corral, my spirits rose as only a few small calves fit the bill. I heaved a sigh of relief. Should be easy. And short.

I glanced around for the wooden chute to pin the calves, but didn't see one. So it was no surprise our jobs were calf wrestling.

With Frank at the front end of the calf and me at the rear, on a signal we grabbed the calf's legs, lifted, and slammed it on its side onto the ground, dust flying, knocking the breath out of it. Dropping on my butt, I jammed my boot against the animal's bottom leg, pushed it forward as hard as I could, while pulling the top leg back, immobilizing the calf. Frank did the same to the front legs.

Frank said, "Don't let go…until it's been…ugh…branded, and Luann injects…the blackleg serum."

We settled into a rhythm, doing a dozen small calves. Then the little calves started getting bigger. When the next one leaped up, bawling piteously, Frank wiped his forehead with the back of his glove saying, "Those yearlings are a little bigger. Didn't get to them last year."

About a dozen brutish yearlings remained, each the size of a hippopotamus, with rippling thigh muscles and horns that gleamed menacingly in the sunlight.

Now each "calf" was a battle. Despite our best efforts, they were big and strong to fight being seared with a hot iron, pricked with a needle, or having their horns--or other parts clipped off. I was getting sore from getting thumped by muscular legs and sharp hooves as they wriggled and kicked and bawled and mooed.

The next calf blew out a loud and odiferous poop all over my leg. Connie laughed, and said with a big grin, "Getting pooped yet?" I couldn't help but laugh with him.

I must have relaxed my grip on the next calf's legs for a second while the branding iron and needle were applied. The calf bucked and the branding iron skidded off its rump onto my pants, scorching them. I smelled burnt cloth. But luckily no burnt skin. A second later I was shocked to feel the sting of a needle in my knee.

LuAnn's mouth opened in a stunned O. She withdrew a half-depressed plunger. She apologized, but I'd already been inoculated.

By the time we finished, my knee had puffed up, and remained stiff for a week.

As a would-be writer, I was always looking for new experiences to write about. Branding cattle was definitely one of them.

And I suspect I'm immune to blackleg.

The Joys of Motorcycling

My first motorized vehicle was a used 150 Honda Motorcycle, which I bought in 1964 for $100. I was deliriously happy to have my own vehicle. The first day my brother Ron hopped on back, and we started tooling around town. On the road near the armory I hit a patch of loose gravel. The motorcycle swayed, and turned sideways, tossing us off. We slid and both suffered gravel burns but nothing more serious. But Ron would not remount, walking the ten blocks home. And he never rode again.

Our family rarely left town, except a couple of rare trips at night, after my step-dad finished his long workday. So I never knew what the landscape west of Wishek was like. Until getting my motorcycle.

For variety I drove the 33 miles west to Linton a couple of times. On the way I marveled at the beauty of the hilly landscape, green and rich, including several flat-topped mesas, which I had never seen before.

Those treks convinced me that I needed a more powerful bike. Like a Honda 305. But it was too expensive, so I settled for a used Kawasaki 250 motorcycle. That was more like it!

I took it to college that fall, where a couple of us motored to a café early several mornings for breakfast. A great time.

If I wanted to go home, and no car of Wishekites was headed that way, I cranked up my motorcycle, stuffed newspapers inside my clothes on my chest and up my arms to ward off the cold, and drove the 90 miles to Wishek. The wind whistled pass me, and rattled the newspapers while cold air shooting by froze me. By the time I got to my destination, my entire body tingled.

That's why I began trailing semis. If I got about a dozen feet behind a speeding semi, the wind was negligible. Plus the mass of the semi sucked me along. I never thought of the danger. Besides, I thought, I was always wearing a helmet.

That summer on my motorcycle I explored the little towns around Valley City, and drove on country roads. One time I zipped around a curve where the turn of the gravel road was hidden, and immediately ahead of me appeared a barbed-wire fence across the road. Only one thing to do: lay the machine on its side, hoping to create enough friction to stop. Kind of worked. But barbs on the wire sliced my pants leg open--and my leg.

At the emergency room they closed the six-inch wound with plastic stitches, and gave me a tetanus shot.

A couple of years later I ended up in the hospital for non-motorcycle-related knee surgery. My roommate was a young guy in because of--you guessed it--a motorcycle accident. Hurt badly. Seeing him suffer made me think. Could that happen to me?

A few weeks later driving on a four-lane road in Jamestown, the car ahead of me in the left lane signaled right. I sped up to go around him on the left, just as he turned--not right, but left. In front of me. I had to swing wide into the opposite lane and jam on the brakes so we didn't collide. If another car had been in that lane coming toward me, I probably wouldn't be writing this today. Scared the heck out of me, and I thought more and more about getting hurt on my bike.

I realized only I could control my actions. And motorcycles are not always easy to see, because of their size, but because it's easy to speed with a motorcycle.

I loved riding motorcycle, the power, the breeze in my face, the sound, the acceleration, turning on a dime, the cheap gas--all the wonders the little machine offered.

But it was time. On the sad day when I finally sold my Kawasaki motorcycle, I cried. But I knew it was the best and healthiest option for me to do.

UFO Sighting at Green Lake

The summer of my junior year in college I was home when Wayne, my eighth-grade brother, was peering into his telescope again. He said, "Billy, look at this! Look!"

"What?"

"Something odd!"

So I looked into the lens of his telescope. And saw a distant object hovering in the sky southeast of town. "Helicopter?" I guessed.

"No rotors."

At my next look, the distant object turned, and I saw a kite-shaped object with flashing lights around its perimeter, different colors cascading along each edge--red, blue, yellow, green. With a thick tube hanging beneath it. "A blimp?"

"Who owns a blimp around here?"

He could hardly stand still. "I think its a UFO!"

Just what I'd been thinking. UFOs had recently been in the news again. Wayne called classmates, and his science teacher, Mr. Douglas. They came over, and when they looked through the telescope they were as puzzled as the rest of us.

"UFO?" one of the kids said.

I called my friend Doug, and told him about it. "Where is it?" he asked. "Let's chase it!"

Not exactly what I had in mind. But 10 minutes later we were barreling east in his 1953 Studebaker into the deep rolling hills of glacial outwash sediment. I worried about being abducted; we'd heard stories about people who had, and were never the same afterwards.

As we got nearer to it on Highway 13 we realized it must be near Green Lake. So we turned onto the gravel road towards the water, and the dot had grown to dollar-size, and was now suspended only about 100 feet above the center of Green Lake, which was four miles long. A long silvery tube hung down into the water.

"What are they doing?" I said.

"Beats me."

Seconds later, the flashing lights went solid, and the tube glinted as it tumbled into the lake. One second the UFO hovered above the water; the next second it was gone. The sky was empty.

"Holy mackerel," Doug said. "Did you see that?"

Dumbfounded, I could only nod.

Over the years I've wondered what that UFO was doing. Was it carrying out reconnaissance? Checking the lake's depth? Performing experiments? Testing for nutrients? Loading ballast or drinking water? Sucking up bullheads and perch and carp for a tasty interstellar meal?

Or something more nefarious, like adding chemicals? Or bacteria? Or alien fish to breed with ours?

Or something that has yet to play out in the future? The possibilities are endless.

"Nobody's going to believe us," I said. Doug nodded.

We don't possess any blurry photos, or evidence of the long silver tube. Did they intentionally dump it? Or did it accidentally come loose? Or any other evidence, except the memories of that strange object hovering above the lake.

I've never seen UFOs anywhere else. But perhaps the extra terrestrials have been here, tagging our fish or foxes. Who knows?

Perhaps the answer is in Shakespeare's Hamlet saying, "There are more things in heaven and earth, Horatio, than are dreamt of in your philosophy."

Liking School, Loving Teaching

When I was a junior in high school, my postmistress Millie asked, "I don't suppose you're anxious to return to school?"

I answered, "Actually, I am. I like school."

"You do?" she said. "I've never heard that from a kid before."

It was true. I did like school. Of course I would miss the joys of summer--playing baseball at the stadium we built, hunting for fossils in the walls of the ravine across the street from where I lived, tossing a Karo syrup pail with nail holes in the bottom on rope into a pond to catch minnows, searching for arrowheads--generally rousting about town to my heart's content.

But school brought other joys--seeing my farm friends, the black-haired girl I had a crush on, the competitive fun of sports, learning all that new and stimulating information, like why we roll our food in saliva before swallowing it; and what makes a tiny explosion in chemistry (when the teacher wasn't around); even how to finally interpret Shakespeare. A new world, really.

Though my high school teachers were very serious, which generally meant not very creative or fun, I still enjoyed school. The exception for creativity was Mr. Erickson, a first-year English teacher when I was a senior. Unfortunately, his ideas often backfired, like the one where we were all supposed to point out classmate errors of all kinds in class, in speaking, in writings handed back and forth, probably even in whispers, and have them listed on a wall chart for all to see. Not hard to imagine how fast that deteriorated.

I continued my love of school by pursuing teaching as my career. I was determined to make English interesting for my students. Some were basic activities, like reading parts in plays, or listening to famous poetry read by the poet, but others were more creative.

For example, after reading a piece on orienteering, I took a tenth-grade class out to hunt for items I'd buried earlier in an area called the sand hills--pens, a couple of half dollars, an old shoe.

After reading *Country of the Blind,* the entire class was blindfolded. Meanwhile all the desks were moved helter-skelter, and students with their masks on had to find theirs by the feel of what they'd left on the desk. Lots of bumping going on.

I asked students from other classes to slip in and brush feathers or a spot of air or mist of water on masked students to show that in a blind world you never knew what you might run into.

I also concocted a blindfolded scavenger hunt, including one where a student had to find a full can of his favorite pop which I'd placed on the front bumper of a teacher's car. The student returned frustrated. "I can't find it!" he said. The teacher had left to pick up something he'd forgotten at home.

The most memorable lesson was in showing students how to build tension in writing. I took them out to an abandoned house a mile out of town and asked them to imagine a murderer in the house searching for them. Was he upstairs? With my hand on the upstairs doorknob at the high point of the story, I ripped the door open and a student I'd sent up onto the steps earlier before we got there leaped out at them, shrieking. Pandemonium ensued for a couple of seconds.

These methods might not be allowed in schools today, but they worked for me. Former students still remember with smiles the abandoned house, the snake, even "being blind."

It makes me glad to know they enjoyed parts of school, even if they couldn't answer "Yes" to Millie the postmistress' question, "Glad to be back in school?"

Farm Work Is Problematic

Growing up in a small agricultural village meant that sooner or later while in high school I would toil on farms to earn extra money. And I did: plowing, discing, picking rock (a loathsome job), erecting grain bins, cutting hay, hauling bales, milking cows, manuring barns, and most problematic, harvesting.

Harvesting, the farmer's hopes for yearly nirvana, was problematic for me because it was boring. For example, driving the grain truck. While my boss combined the crop, I was forced to sit in a sun-hot stifling ton-and-a-half truck in a field amidst blowing chaff and no air conditioning. My sole job was to watch for my boss' signal that his combine's grain tank was full, and he needed to empty it into my truck box.

Simple, right? But tedious. On day two I brought Ray Bradbury's *The Martian Chronicles,* and laid it open against the upper half of the steering wheel so as I read I only needed to glance up and out the windshield to note the progress of the combine.

Which worked for a while. Except the book transported me into an enthralling new world, and I missed my boss' signals a couple of times by about a minute. Not too drastic. Until one time I was so wrapped up in the beauty of Bradbury's words, and the story, that I missed his signals for at least a good five minutes.

To try to get my attention he stood atop the grain tank waving his arms to make a bigger target. But since I never looked up, I never saw him. Boy, was he mad. That cured me. I still read a half page or so at a time, but looked up constantly.

Taking the loaded truck to the elevator was another ordeal, having to wait in line behind a dozen other trucks all needing to unload. The going was slow, so I read again. Because I was a newbie at driving a big truck with a full load of grain, it was too easy for me to humiliate myself by killing the straight stick in front of everybody when driving only a few inches, and I wanted to wait until the truck ahead of me was at least three feet or so away, instead of trying to inch ahead like the trucks in front of me.

However, other drivers behind me weren't going to give me a break. If I didn't move a millimeter ahead instantly, some trucks behind me honked, so anxious to move inches ahead even though it would be many minutes before they would get to unload.

Another problem was my boss had a reputation for cheating, which I didn't know. And when the elevator workers started poking in the wheat in my box with their shovels--which they hadn't done to the two trucks ahead of me, at least--I kept asking what they were doing, and they rolled their eyes, doubtless thinking I was in on the scam.

Finally, one stuck his shovel in and said, "Here it is." "It" was wet grain, hidden near the back so it would cascade out as soon as the box on the truck was raised. My boss had added water to increase its weight, which would make the load heavier and garner a bigger payment. But wet grain--caught--lowered the price of the entire load of grain. My boss was mad at that, too.

I discovered how difficult being a farmer could be. So I was more than thankful that farm work ended for me.

Boss Hawg at School

One year during the last week of school I took my ninth-grade English class out into area sand hills to practice orienteering, or the competitive locating of hidden objects. We'd read a short essay on the practice.

I had gone out earlier and buried prizes for them to track down using my written directions: "20 paces west from the cut-down dead bushes."

On the way back to the bus, we came upon a dead hog-nosed snake, long as a pencil, twice as thick, on its back, white belly up. I picked it up. Its chin was a sharp, flat up-sloping plate that gave it a vaguely hoggish look, yet seemed to be smiling, as though it had just played a trick and you didn't know it.

Which was true. Western hog-nosed snakes, *Heterodon nasicus nasicus,* "are notorious for playing dead when threatened," says *Wikipedia.* The vibrations of 40 marching feet probably threatened the little beast, as in the bus a few miles down the road, a girl screamed. "Eek! Mr. V.! You've got a snake crawling on your neck!"

Sure enough. I had grabbed the little faker amidst the unsettled murmurs of my students. Collecting a snake: just another Vossler weirdness.

Boss Hawg was the first western hog-nosed snake I had ever seen. Over the summer he and I developed a daily ritual. After my breakfast, I pushed small chunks of lunch meat down his throat with the eraser end of a pencil. Sated, Boss Hawg curled contentedly around my right index finger, a boon companion, while I grasped a notebook with my remaining fingers, and wrote with my other hand. If he got antsy, I dropped him into my shirt pocket.

On the Sunday before the start of the new school year, I went to the school to organize my classroom, forgetting that I'd slipped Boss Hawg into my shirt pocket. When I leaned over the table to grab a stapler from the communal tool box in the teacher's lounge, he evidently fell--or leaped--out.

Back home, I couldn't find Boss Hawg. Not unusual. Sometimes he got loose and skittered across the carpet, hell-bent for freedom. He crawled under the loose edge of the carpet against the wall, making a break for it. Usually I found him in a couple of minutes.

But not this time. I searched my writing room, kitchen, bedroom, bathroom--everywhere. No Boss Hawg.

That first Monday I was teaching when a loud knock interrupted my class. The superintendent stepped in, dangling Boss Hawg from his fingers. "This yours?" he asked.

A teacher's aide--deathly afraid of snakes, of course--had scrabbled in the communal box for a pen, and picked up a snake instead. Quite a troubling monumental surprise. She screamed, dropped Boss Hawg, and ran from the room, hyperventilating.

Though I'd taught two of her children, and played amateur sports with two others, and regularly frequented their grocery store across the street, Betty was never the same towards me after that.

If she saw me in the halls, she scurried into a room, or turned and fled. If we ever spoke again during my four years there, it was cursory and absolutely necessary.

I couldn't blame her.

I kept my connection with Boss Hawg until one day he disappeared in our house, and we never did find him.

The Case of the Missing Mallards

One particular year of my coaching career could be described like the old movie, *The Good, the Bad, and the Ugly*.

I was a first-year varsity coach in a tiny North Dakota hamlet whose psyche was bound up in the success of the boys' high school basketball team. Not really unusual in those small towns. But I failed to understand its intensity.

So I was surprised at halftime of my first game when a couple of parents stepped into the locker room to offer suggestions on how I could coach better. Co-coaching was a new concept to me, but I listened politely. A mistake, as different parents showed up in the locker room in future games to advise me during halftime.

That got my goat. From then on I declared halftime inviolate from parents, which did not set well with them.

Except we won our first 11 games in a tough conference, far outstripping expectations, making me an overnight coaching genius.

That was the good.

Until we lost the next 11 in a row. Obviously the bad. I faced grumbling and angry words from some parents, especially when I inserted two players from my stellar B-squad team as varsity starters.

Amidst that 11-game loss string came the ugly. In the Stutsman County tournament, we got down a dozen points against a very good team and couldn't get any closer. They were simply better.

Then one of my players sprained his ankle in the fourth quarter, and lay sprawled on the floor clutching his leg. The other team had the ball, so I couldn't call time out. Yet the game continued.

I was irate. In a full-length leg cast with a torn Achilles tendon, I hobbled out and pointed at my player with a crutch and screamed at the ref to stop the game.

"He's hurt! Can't you see?"

He turned and poked me hard in the chest, making me stagger back. "We cannot," he poked, I staggered, "stop a game," poke, stagger, "for an injury." Poke, stagger, until I flopped back down hard onto the bench. He said if I got up again he would toss me out, crutches and all.

When it was our ball, I finally called time out. My player was helped off the floor. A minute later, the buzzer rang to resume play. The ref looked at the my bench and asked who I was subbing.

"No one," I said. "We'll go with four."

His mouth dropped open. "Ooookay," he said.

As our players took positions on the floor, some in the crowd yelled, "You've only got four players out there, only four!"

Two minutes later a Mallard player fouled out. When the game resumed, only three Mallard players stepped on the floor. A buzz went through the crowd as they tried to comprehend why this idiot coach played only three players.

I wasn't excited about it either, but the reasoning was simple: our B-squad team was undefeated. Five of those players were on the varsity, sitting on the bench beside me.

But B-squad players were allowed only one tournament a year. If I played any of them for even one second, they lost their eligibility for the entire B-squad tournament. A no-brainer for me.

After the game ended, my detractors were madder than hornets. My explanation fell on deaf ears. I'd humiliated their city.

The sports editor of the *Jamestown Sun* asked why I'd played only three for two minutes, so I told him. "Sounds logical," he said.

After he quoted me in an article titled *The Case of the Missing Mallards*, I figured everybody would be mollified. Especially when we won the B-squad tournament.

But they weren't. At the end of the year the school board tried to fire me. Unsuccessfully. But I loved the kids and my fellow teachers, so I taught there five more years, coaching three. Fortunately I never had to use fewer than five players in a game again.

The Achilles Heel

On January 7, 1970, I wrapped tape tightly around my left Achilles tendon, and though it ached, I wasn't going to miss playing in that night's big amateur basketball game.

When a person runs or jumps, the Achilles tendon, the largest and strongest in the body, is subjected to a load of up to ten times one's body weight. So it is no wonder that it can tear, as with football quarterbacks Aaron Rodgers and Kirk Cousins.

And me. Twice.

In the first quarter of that game, I stole the ball, raced down the floor and when a defender cut in front of me, I leaped and drilled the shot--just as my mortal enemy from the other team kicked my Achilles from behind.

Or so I thought. I collapsed, grabbing my Achilles, turned and saw him immediately behind me. I was livid. I called him a naughty name or two. He looked very surprised. I couldn't believe the refs didn't call a foul. I yammered at them as I was helped off the floor. One of our substitute players loaded me in the car.

In the emergency room the doctor glanced at my limp left foot, said, "Torn Achilles tendon. Felt like you got kicked, right?"

"I did get kicked."

"No, you didn't. You thought you did. Everybody thinks so."

I frowned. Was I wrong?

"When do you want to do surgery?"

"Surgery?" I said, aghast. "My team needs me. I have to be back playing again after halftime."

He chuckled. "Not hardly. A bit more serious than that, I'm afraid."

On NPR recently a doctor said, "A torn Achilles tendon looks like a bowl of spaghetti."

Each torn spaghetti cord on the bottom must be connected to one at the top. Which explains my 104 stitches connecting the many pieces of my torn left Achilles together.

Under the influence of anesthesia, I was later told, I kept the young nurses in stitches. So much so that a couple were disciplined for spending too much time in my room, where my hilarious ministrations kept my roommate from sleeping.

I was out of it, and don't remember what I said. Who knew I was so funny?

My cast ran from the top of my thigh down to just before my toes, and itched worst at my inaccessible knee. With crutches, I got around as best as I could, and returned a week later to teaching English. No substitute teachers were available, but my students had done the work in my sub plans anyway.

Each doctor visit after that elicited hope the cast would be removed. Instead the answer was always, "Nope! A few more weeks." Achilles ruptures were rare, little was known how to deal with them, and some doctors thought we who tore our Achilles might never walk properly again. Much less play sports at a high level, which was top priority for me. So I worried.

Finally 18 weeks later, the magic day came. The doctor cut the cast off revealing an ugly skinny leg with three-inch-long hairs. For the first time I saw he had inserted a wire connected to a washer on the bottom of my foot, running up eight inches through the center of the Achilles to stabilize it. At the top, the wire protruded out of the side of my leg above my ankle, where it was folded over.

With a pliers he clipped the folded wire, grabbed the washer with the pliers, and without warning, jerked hard and yanked the wire out. Pain radiated through the middle of my Achilles all the way down. "Yeow!" I said.

After examining the dozen scars from the stitches on the inside of my ankle, he grabbed my toes, and said, "How does this FEEL?" he shouted as he forced my foot up as hard as he could." Which hurt, but the Achilles held.

The Achilles remained stiff for months, and I needed to stretch it every morning. As it mended, for a couple of months I played sports gingerly, always worried about re-tearing it.

Physical therapy and rehabbing did not exist, so I slowly increased my strength and flexibility by running every day, playing softball, baseball, basketball, and tennis carefully, until the stiffness disappeared and I forget the injury, and returned to normal.

But I was lucky. First baseman Bill White of the St. Louis Cardinals, an eight-time all-star who tore his Achilles the same day I tore mine, needed painkillers every day--and tearing the tendon ended his baseball career.

Alpha and Omega

I poked death in the eye by challenging the roaring subzero wind of a prairie blizzard. On one good leg. And crutches. For a mile. With twilight bleeding away into the great northern darkness.

Not intentionally. Coming home mid-Saturday afternoon from errands in Jamestown, the road disappeared in swirls of snow, and my car skidded into a curve, burying the front end in a mountainous drift in the ditch. A mile from the farm where I lived. No cellphone in those days.

Prairie folk are seldom foolish concerning weather--except when worshiping at the shrine of their little-town basketball, often the sole winter excitement in a dreary white-whipped world. The high school team I coached was 11-0, playing our fierce rival that evening for the conference lead, and everyone in our rabid little school would expect the game to be played. What was a little snow? And wind? They were farmers, inured to bad weather. My team was playing well, so I was eager for the contest, too.

My superintendent was gone on a family emergency, leaving me to make the call. Now with a blizzard kicking up, the game had to be postponed. Despite dangerous wind chills, on crutches, I had to get to a telephone.

I tried backing up out of the ditch. Immobile as a glacier. I slammed the steering wheel with my hands. *Stay with your vehicle* was what I'd always been told. But I had no choice. The kids had to be notified for sure that the game would be postponed.

I turned off the ignition. The wind yowled, rattling snow against the windows. I bundled up, secured a sock over my bare toes peeking out of my full-length cast for my torn Achilles, and heaved a great breath. *Here goes nothing.* I hopped out into a whirling white world of relentless wind, blinding me with rocketing snow.

I shuddered. Colder than I'd thought. Just what Jack London's character thought in *To Build a Fire*. He froze to death. I cursed, set the crutches under my armpits, slammed the door, and crabbed into the polar blast. A mile. A good hour, if I was lucky.

After a hundred staggering steps, the frigid fingers of the delving wind exposed my every weakness: tingling ears, aching fingertips, frozen cocoon of cast clutching from my crotch to my stinging toes, with the exposed end of a piece of wire inside my leg holding my torn Achilles tendon in place, shooting jolts of fiery pain into my heel.

Set manageable goals, I always told my players. So, 20 steps, rest. Now, 25. Rest. Twenty again, the crutches creaking each time. Slog on. Many steps later I peered back into the gathering ominous darkness. Turn around? No, I could easily miss the car and crutch into oblivion. I gritted my teeth, and wobbled onward into the gloom. Once the road disappeared in snow or darkness...no, I wouldn't think about it.

Twenty minutes later, shivering, I hallucinated: a car by the side of the road? A combine? A bull? Had I stumbled into a field?

So when the giant hand of wind smacked me in the back, propelling me five feet forward, I was confounded. My thoughts were treacle. I shook my head. I'd heard of people hallucinating when they got really cold. Or falling asleep and freezing to death. Then I realized the wind was now behind me!

Deliriously, with my clutches I levered myself forward, the wind throwing me seven, 10 feet at a time, five times faster than before. I flew, one leg and crutches thumping down, struggling for balance, leaping forward again, again, again, my world a narrow swath of fading white.

My hands were lumps of ice, breath shattered out of my chest, the wild wind whirled and howled around me as the shadow of darkness seeped into the light.

Eventually, exhausted beyond belief, I stopped, yearning to plop down into a snow bank for a short nap. No, no, danger! Danger! Couldn't think clearly. Hypothermia was setting in. Go, go!

I staggered on, and five steps later bumped into something. Couldn't see it in the Stygian darkness. I leaned against it to keep upright. What was it? Dimly I realized, a mailbox! Could it be our own?

I hobbled sideways, stabbing my crutch into the snow. Didn't realize I was sobbing until it poked the solid driveway.

Keening, I turned into the driveway. I can make it! I wiped tears with my cold sleeve, and lurched toward the dim house. Stay on the road!

The wind dropped off, sheared away by trees alongside the driveway that I felt rather than saw.

Hours later, it seemed, the yard light winked through the eddying snow. The shadowy bulk of the house loomed. My hands wouldn't work. I kicked the door, violently, Bam Bam Bam. No feeling in my toes. I kicked again. Loretta, my roommate's mother, jerked it open. Her jaw dropped.

"Phone!" I blurted through frozen lips, "Postpone!"

I staggered in, asked her to dial, and hold the phone to my ear. I spoke hoarsely. I gasped. The telephone tree was begun. No game tonight. I could stop imagining my ill-dressed players and cheerleaders (teens, after all) sliding off the road, stumbling blindly through the bitter cold, to be claimed by the same impartial fury of London's story.

One by one Loretta unwrapped my fingers from my crutches. She removed my gloves, rubbed my white hands, thrust them under warm water.

I groaned and cried, in pain. And in relief.

The Short Happy Life of Mr. Kelly

The only time a dog ever bit me, I had to have him tested for rabies.

A black lab, Mr. Kelly entered my life when I was living alone on a farm near Woodworth, North Dakota, where I taught English.

Each morning when I left, Mr. Kelly sat in the driveway, panting with excitement, as though saying, "See you this afternoon!" Each day he kept his promise, in the driveway, his tongue lolling. When I got home he threw himself at me, whining delightedly.

I naïvely thought Mr. Kelly stayed home while I was gone. But a nearby farmer said Mr. Kelly had been chasing his cattle. But Mr. Kelly was always home when I got back. So I figured that was not possible. Soon three other farmers had the same complaint, but I really thought they had the wrong black lab.

One afternoon Mr. Kelly wasn't waiting for me. A farmer called, saying he had my dog, who had been harassing his cattle. "Tie him up," he said, "or someone might hurt him."

So I tied him up. Which broke his heart. He was miserable.

One Tuesday he broke away and wouldn't be caught. He danced around. Freedom! Yay! I could see it in his eyes.

That evening he was lethargic, sickly, no interest in food. As I read in bed he curled up warmly against my side. All night he thrashed and whined. Something was seriously wrong.

Wednesday I took him to a veterinarian. "Looks like some kind of poison," the veterinarian said. "We can help critters poisoned with strychnine, but this isn't strychnine. He'll have to work it out himself." I brought my poor dog home.

Thursday morning Mr. Kelly was worse. He stumbled, eyes unfocused, confused, so I took him to school. During lunch several students came out and petted him, and despite the fire raging in his gut, he wagged his tail weakly and offered his head to be petted.

That evening while doing house things, I felt Mr. Kelly's pleading eyes on me as if to say. "Why don't you do something?" He drank a little water, but ignored his food. Would he be dead by morning?

Friday morning the bright light of starvation burned in his eyes. No food in four days. His ribs showed. I sat with him on the couch and whispered endearments, and petted him. Maybe the last time?

But somehow he hung on. After school, he greeted me, wobbling and jerking, and nudged me with his head so I would pet him.

I checked his food. A miracle! He'd eaten! Not much, but he'd eaten! He was feeling better! I fed him more, and he ate that. I was elated. He was going to get well!

In the middle of that night he kicked me hard, twice. I turned and petted him unfortunately on his stomach. He yelped and bit me on the arm. He was warm and feverish, but an hour later he was cooler. The fever had broken!

In the morning I touched him, and jerked back my hand. He was cold and rigid. I rolled over and laid my head on him, and I cried. My boon companion was gone.

That morning I received two telephone calls. The first from an irate woman in town who said my dog was pawing through her trash.

"That's quite a trick," I said angrily, "Considering he's laying beside me dead."

The second was from the veterinarian. He asked how Mr. Kelly was doing. When I told him he had died, and bit me, drawing blood, he urged me to bring him in so they could send his head in to make sure that he wasn't rabid. The final indignity.

For weeks afterwards every time I heard a sound in the house I turned and expected to see Mr. Kelly. Every time, my heart broke, because he was no longer there.

Cause and Effect

At a party one evening in Jamestown, N.D., many years ago, a man I didn't recognize kept glancing at me and frowning in an unpleasant manner. An enemy through sports? Brother of a student who'd received F's? Sibling of a basketball or softball player who didn't get enough playing time on a team I coached? I couldn't come up with anything.

So I shrugged and continued chatting with the host. A few minutes later Mr. Frown's chair suddenly scraped as he bolted out of it and stormed over towards me, the light of comprehension flicking on in his eyes.

"You!" he said, jabbing me in the chest. "It was you!"

Five months earlier I had awakened on a Monday morning, sick with a bad cold and cough for the third consecutive day. I called in to my disappointed superintendent, and out of habit checked the outdoor temperature--minus 32 Fahrenheit. Yeek! I shrugged. North Dakota. I bundled up for the doctor's. Outside a frigid north wind snatched my white balloons of breath away, and slapped me icily on the cheeks and forehead.

I trudged to my frost-inundated car. None of us in the small apartment building had a garage, so it was no great surprise that my vehicle refused to go. "No nooo oh oh oh!" Wouldn't turn over.

So I knocked on the door of my girlfriend's apartment, and asked to borrow her car. She was hesitant, but finally agreed. "But be careful!" she admonished. "It's the only one I've got."

"Ha ha!" I said. "Thank you. I'll return it in one piece."

I was sick and tired so I didn't clean off more than a small area of the windshield sufficient to peek out. Without incident, I drove to the doctor's, coughing and hacking--not the car, me--got fixed up and set free.

I drove Gwen's car two blocks to a stop sign, peering through the minimally-cleaned windshield. I was anxious to return home and crawl into a nice warm bed, so after a quick inconclusive glance back and forth, on a wing and a prayer I punched the accelerator, turned left, and a second later, wham! The front of Gwen's car leaped up.

Hearing the hissing of the radiator of another car, I realized I'd struck a vehicle I hadn't seen. Then at the top of my frosted windshield I saw an ominous sight: a rotating light flared on, blanketing my windshield red blue red blue red. Followed by a whining siren.

My first thought was, how did the cops get here so fast? No matter. I was angry at the other driver, so jumped out of Gwen's car, angry that I was going to owe money for a ticket, angry that I was going to owe Gwen money for damages to her car, money I could ill-afford, so I yelled at the other driver, "Why don't you drive in your own lane?"

"What?" he screamed. "Look! Your car is in my lane."

And so it was. Halfways.

That's when I noticed his Jamestown police uniform, and the pieces of the incident fell into one coherent picture. Probably because of my obvious coughing and hacking illness, our business was concluded quickly.

Over with in my mind until the party, where this Jamestown policeman was heatedly reading me the riot act, jabbing his finger at me. "That was a brand new squad car that you wrecked. We'd just gotten it that week!" His voice was rising. "And here it is six months later." Higher. "And we still can't get the parts to fix it!" The edges of his lips were spittle-covered.

I mumbled a few words in apology, and skulked away out to my vehicle. And though it didn't need it, as a reminder I sprayed windshield solution and cleaned off my windshield before I slid in. Lesson learned.

Paranoid About Praise

The Germans-from-the Ukraine culture in which I grew up was paranoid about praise. Basically, nobody ever praised anybody about anything because "They might get a big head, or get too big for their britches." Every nail had to be pounded flat.

For example, one time when I was 6, Bob, 8, Ron, 4, and Mom were walking on the sidewalk toward home when a neighbor stopped us and said, "Alma, you have such nice boys."

Mom quickly squelched those kind words with, "Yeah, but you should see them at home!"

Because of this constraint against praise, all I ever heard was criticism, thus believed I was never doing anything right. So I tried to do everything perfectly, which created its own set of problems.

In the same vein, my father was a war hero in 1944, which I didn't learn until 50 years later, because people were paranoid about praise. I wrote about this story in the *War Hero* chapter in my first memoir, *Days of Wonder*.

His story was published in a 1946 issue of *The Wishek Star*. Mom said nobody told us about it because they thought we would get big heads, bragging that "My dad was a war hero."

One time I let that general lack of praise overthrow me. Our amateur basketball team was playing in the championship of the North Dakota State Class B amateur tournament in Bismarck. Early in the game I stole the ball and shot a layup. When the ball dropped through the hoop, the announcer screamed, "Vossssssler scores!" At that time those were the most beautiful words I'd ever heard.

That set me off. I couldn't believe how that made me feel. And I wanted to feel that way again.

Normally I was a team player, but after that giddiness all I thought about was myself, wanting to hear those words again. So in the next few minutes, I shot four times, never checking if any teammates were open. I made two, hearing my name so wonderfully yelled again, and missed two (one was blocked) before I came to my senses.

We lost the game by one point. Who knows how it would have ended if I had passed the ball instead of getting it blocked?

So while I covet praise, I am learning how to share it, by praising those I love, no matter how small the praise is.

Running A Bookstore

My Books 'N Things bookstore in Jamestown provided me with many learning opportunities that I could never have predicted.

One day a fortyish woman entered my store, tears streaming down her face as she sobbed, "Liz and Dick, Liz and Dick, I can't believe it," and while muttering and crying about the divorce, rummaged through the new book racks.

A half-hour later she brought $34 worth of new paperback and hardcover books up to the counter--a huge purchase in 1972-- and paid by check. Earlier I'd seen her come out of the bank kitty-corner across the street, so I was more than surprised a couple of days later when her check bounced. I discovered that after closing her account in the bank, she walked across the street to my store to essentially steal my books, then skedaddled to places unknown.

With book profits at 25%, I had to sell a hundred dollars worth of books just to break even.

Another character stopped in the store like clockwork once a week at five minutes before closing time. He perused books, until 20 minutes past closing. But he never bought anything.

Until one day he lugged a pile of 10 new and used books and stacked them on the counter. I began to tally what he owed. He retrieved a five from his billfold, and placed it on the counter. "You don't have to total that. I'll give you five dollars for the lot."

I looked at him in astonishment and shook my head. "I'm like any other store," I said, "The price is clearly marked on all of the books, and the total you owe me is $25. That's the cost."

He gazed at me in surprise. "You mean you won't give a good customer like me a deal?"

"Good customer?" I said. The clock read 20 minutes after six, and I'd kept the store open late just for him. It got me fuming.

Maybe I'd had a bad day because I said, "You've never... Get out of my store, and don't ever come back." I pointed at the door. He left and never did return.

But the bookstore provided me with tons of good moments to, like seeing the joy on the faces of people as they purchased books, or exchanged their used ones for cash or other used books, as Books 'N Things had used and new books.

Every two weeks an obviously-poor woman bought a single Harlequin Romance from the shelves, so as she perused, we chatted back and forth, about the world and difficulties of her life.

One day she asked for my mother's address. I asked her why. She smiled and said she wanted to tell my mother what a nice son she had raised. Praise!

Which Valeria did, writing letters to my mother in a large hand, praising me, and despite her very limited resources, adding a small gift for Mom each time. It reminded me of the Biblical story of the widow's mite, giving freely when she had next to nothing.

My bookstores never made much money, but they made me an emotionally-richer person.

The Road Not Taken

Each one of us has taken a proverbial "Road less traveled by" which altered our life forever--for good or ill.

One of my diverging roads occurred the day I drove five and a half hours to Sioux Falls, South Dakota, to apply for a teaching job. Looking back, my main reason was to escape a bad relationship. I was sure if I taught elsewhere, she wouldn't follow.

Not 8,800 miles. Not to Australia.

The recruiter and I met in a skyscraper in Sioux Falls where he asked me questions about my nine-year teaching career thus far, and seemed most interested in my time at Standing Rock Sioux Indian Reservation at Fort Yates, North Dakota, wondering how I'd felt teaching in a school of different-race students. I said "It had its challenges, but I liked it a lot. I liked smaller settings," He said that would work just fine, because I would be quartered out of Sydney, probably somewhere in the Outback, with many smaller schools. We chatted back and forth, he examined my references, closed the file, and said I was hired.

I asked him about playing basketball, and he said there were hoops. Outdoors. That did not sound very encouraging, so I began having second thoughts. Playing amateur sports, especially basketball, was a huge part of my life.

I'd been musing my emigrating would resemble my forebears leaving Germany to move to the Ukraine in the 1760s, and to the United States in the 1890s, which had always intrigued me. What was it like to forsake your country for a new one?

Huge differences existed between me and them, of course-- they spoke German, I spoke English, though I had some trouble with my recruiter's Australian accent, and thought I would take a while to adjust. I had no clue what "Eydeeth" meant until by his gestures and continuing to say "Eydeenth" I realized he was indicating the floors in the skyscraper, so he was saying "eighteenth," though our skyscraper didn't have that many floors. Other words were difficult to understand too.

My ancestors moved to where they knew other Germans-from-the-Ukraine, but I would be all alone. More second thoughts.

As our interview ended, I took the contract and information and returned to North Dakota to think about what it would be like to move into the Australian Outback.

Back home I read up on the Outback, and discovered I would be teaching indigenous students--of a different race, thus his more pointed questions about teaching on the reservation, and I would be in the challenging physical territory of the 4,000-foot-high Blue Mountains, with towns like Bullaburra, Wintumba, and Batoomba–and I was a plains guy who loved the wide-open spaces. More second thoughts.

Finally I decided against Australia, at least then. The contract opening ran for a full year. I faced my girlfriend problem by breaking up with her, though it caused discomfort through the school year as she was a special needs teacher in my classroom several days a week.

Every three months Australia contacted me to see if I had reconsidered. I honestly thought about it each time, but decided Australia didn't work for me. A year later, they made their last overture to me, saying they were sad because I would have made a very good teacher for those Australian children.

The process made me appreciate the huge courage it took my people to leave villages where they had grown up, where they had known their friends and neighbors for many years, and understood how life worked in the community, to embark on a foray into an entirely new--and very dangerous world of the Ukraine, where 4,000 of the German transfers were carried off into slavery or murdered by marauding Ukrainian groups. That was followed by the safe but very challenging new life in the United States and North Dakota.

I sometimes still wonder how differently my life would have been had I had taken that other road.

Mountain Challenge

The summer day was clear when my cousin Tim and I set out to climb one of the mountains in the Pryor chain in Montana. A few wispy clouds fluffed further back. We parked his pickup next to a 20-foot-wide stream, climbed down the bank and pushed two large bottles of 7-Up deep into the cold water by the bank of the low, sluggish rill. We crossed a small rickety bridge to begin our ascent.

Our climb was an easy walk at first, really--up the foothill, we caught up with each other's lives since we'd seen each other last, 10 years earlier at age 13, before Tim's family moved to Billings.

I stopped often because I was a child of the great drift plains, mesmerized by the towering pillars of rock that continued to appear as we moved up one foothill, then another and another. Then the unfamiliar plant life--lupine, Wyoming big sagebrush, arrowleaf balsamroot, and yucca, which Tim identified for me.

As we climbed, we heard the occasional deep grumble of thunder far away. Four hours later we breasted another rise, and Tim said, breathing hard, "There, the top." Three hundred feet of bare rock, much more sheer and challenging than we'd climbed so far.

Then a slab of black clouds suddenly blotted out the sun. As though driven by the sizzling zigzags of white-hot lightnings, a phalanx of wind, laden with a slanting sheet of cold rain struck us, followed instantly by terrifying cannonades of thunder. The booming echoed off the rocky crags.

We spotted an overhang, and wet and shivering, rode out the storm, lightning crackling feet away, sharp ozone, rain torrents.

When it stopped, we stepped out--and one glance at the peak and its glistening wet, slippery rock stopped us. Too dangerous. Disappointed, we picked our way back.

And found a stream we no longer recognized, a raging torrent boiling at its filled banks. Simultaneously we said, "Where's the bridge?" We gazed up and down the teeming watercourse. It was gone. A few broken wooden posts remained.

"How are we going to get across?" Tim asked.

I shrugged. "We have to swim," I said, gulping.

Tim tossed a stick into the racing current. It jetted away at super speed. "I can't swim that," he said.

"If we took a running jump?" I said.

Tim shook his head. I was glad he said no. I couldn't swim well enough either. But what were our choices?

We'd been gone at least eight hours. The shadows of the mountain were creeping toward us. Tim's pickup, only 40 feet away, mocked us, as though to say, "Have a nice cold night over there!"

With nothing nearby to help, we walked downstream. Around a bend we spotted several downed trees. The shadows deepened as we raced towards them as they lay on the ground in the midst of other dead ones.

We had hope. We would make our own bridge!

We hefted one log over the rushing water toward the other bank. But it was too heavy. And unwieldy. When the end touched the water it was snatched from our puny hands like a stick by an angry giant. We gazed at each other. What if we had tried to swim across?

We hugged the second one tighter, but the rough bark tore our palms as it was ripped away. Only one more, with a large crook at the end, appeared long enough. We nodded. One more shot.

We held the crook upward as we grunted the tree across the breach. Gasping, our muscles quivering, we flipped the crook downward. The end settled on the other bank. We gently laid down our end.

"It worked!" Tim said.

I sat on the makeshift bridge as Tim scampered across on all fours. I followed.

Safe on the other side, we took deep breaths and shook each other's hand. As we walked to the pickup, Tim checked the eroded bank and said, "Rats, we really could have used that 7-Up, huh?"

Softball Almost Stars

Our North Dakota slow-pitch softball team was thrilled to play in the national tournament in Cincinnati, Ohio in early September 1972. We felt like we deserved it. We were good, and we knew it.

We were a powerhouse, winning 70-some games that summer, including 40 wins and eight tournaments in a row, losing only 12 games all summer.

We had a unique team in several ways. All the players grew up in the environs of the little hamlet of Woodworth, population 139--except me, who taught there. Our talented team included a pair of brothers with a relative who was a Gehrig.

We loved the game so much that if we could find a free diamond between tournament games, we played amongst ourselves. Definitely unique.

We liked each other, which translated into a great deal of fun--winning is always fun--but we were small-town and naïve. Our first naïveté was exposed while playing White Bear Lake, Minnesota, which boasted a team loaded with big strapping players, numbers we hadn't seen in North Dakota.

Stubby was pitching that day. After he made a couple of pitches, several players on the White Bear Lake team started yelling, "Step back, pitch, step back!"

When pitching, we stepped forward with one foot, releasing the ball in an underhanded arc no higher than 10 feet above the ground, and then bringing the other foot forward, preparing for balls hit back at us. We'd never heard of stepping back after releasing the ball. So we didn't.

But we had never played a team the quality of WBL, and their hitter quickly showed why pitchers needed to step back. One

WBL player smacked a rocket back onto Stubby's forehead, imprinting the seams of the ball there. Despite that, he kept pitching. I felt lucky I wasn't pitching that day. From then on, we learned it was wise to step back after releasing the ball.

For the trip to the nationals team sponsors bought four new tires for each vehicle willing to drive down to Cincinnati, including my 1972 Mustang. On the way through Wisconsin, on the main highway near a small town, I got picked up for speeding. We were required to drive to the town's police station in the middle of the night and pay a fine. $70. In cash. No receipt offered.

Nearing Chicago, one of our cars pulled off to fill gas. When the driver went into pay, the clerk said, "Oh, that price on the pump is wrong. It's actually double what it shows." What can you do? You pay. Cash. No receipt.

When we got to Cincinnati, we drove around until we found an open diamond, and started practicing. After a while a girl, perhaps 15, sat on the bleachers behind the backstop watching us.

While waiting on deck to take some swings, I asked her some questions, and found out she was homeless. My eyes must have gone as large as dinner-plates. Homeless? People didn't have homes? Including kids? That was mind-boggling.

After the first game, we ate at a restaurant. One teammate, who I realized later couldn't read--ran across a busy four-lane superhighway to eat at McDonald's, where he knew the menu.

Later, we toured a Cincinnati Arboretum, where I was shocked by the number of flowers that existed, way more than my mother had planted when I was growing up.

Small-town kids, we learned many new things on that journey, including that our team was as good as most of the teams there, and deserved to be there. Unfortunately, we got the draw as visiting team two games in a row. We were competitive in both games, but lost in the bottom of the last, or seventh inning, in both.

At the time, I didn't really appreciate the unique opportunity I'd experienced. I suppose I was a little cocky, figuring with all that talent we'd get back there a couple more times.

I learned a lot about life, which I'll never forget. I later learned the national was never to happen again for us.

Thanks For Great Friends

I am grateful this Thanksgiving season for many people in my life, but I want to name two in particular, Jim and Larry, from Woodworth, North Dakota. They have been great friends since 1966, when I started playing for their home town's amateur basketball team.

Soon I also began to play slow-pitch softball with the Woodworth team, and that's really when I got to know Jim and Larry. They played softball brilliantly--their grandmother, or great, was a Gehrig--and took us the National Tournament in 1973.

Soon we lived together summers, and as our lives meshed in sports and general life, I realized how much their ethics and core values lined up with mine.

Keep Your Word. If you sign up for something, your duty is to show up. One summer Jim drove 82 miles every week after a day of work to play softball with our team in the Jamestown league.

Be Positive. From them I learned to be positive. During games they praised players, so we all began to say "Good play," or "Nice shot," not only to our teams, but members of other teams. They taught us also to play fairly, and be good winners and losers.

Choose Good People to Be Around You. Jim populated our softball teams with good people, even some that weren't hugely talented. Still we won 90% of our softball games because camaraderie strengthened our mutual trust.

Find Humor in Life. After games team members retired to our Jamestown house, which did not have enough seating, so guys would lay on the living room floor. Minutes later someone would drop down on the person on the floor and start wrestling. Clint would ref. His best line was, "That hold is illegal in some states. Should be in all." The horseplay and laughter relaxed us all.

With laughter Jim and Larry reminded me (and still do) when I brought a $1 used car tire from a garage sale in Milwaukee back to Jamestown in a van packed with people.

Be Kind. Their philosophy was "Never criticize. If a teammate made a mistake they already know they made it." Once we had one tremendously talented player with a bullet arm and exceptional fielding ability. But he liked to show off--at times by catching pop-ups behind his back. During games. Though he never missed one, Jim quietly took him aside and convinced him that his actions made our team look bad, and he stopped.

When I was producing my *North Dakota Sports Journal* Jim drove down 70 miles from Bismarck to help me put several issues together, working at night while I slept so I could teach the next day.

Always Do Your Best. Jim and Larry, in life, in games, in coaching, never said "win" or "lose," but rather "Do your best." And their championship coaching mirrored that. Even when slightly injured, each of us played as hard as we could.

Visit Friends. Seemed like Jim and Larry knew someone in every town in North Dakota. No matter where they were, people they knew would stop and talk to them, and vice versa. Even at a Minnesota Twins' game in Minneapolis they find people they know.

Take Care of Your Body. In addition to playing sports, we all ran, and I learned a great deal from them about running--although I learned the most from their younger brother Harry, who I taught and coached. I was the only coach in the small school, and knew nothing about running. Harry took me out running and showed me how to become a distance runner: "Never run hard at the end, because that's what you'll remember next time out and will make it more difficult to do your next run."

He knew what he was talking about, as he won several of North Dakota state running titles.

The list of what I learned from Jim and Larry could go on and on. This Thanksgiving season I give thanks for them, because my life is richer because of them.

Baseball's Other Reward

The baseball, a white cowhide-covered spheroid nine inches around, weighs five ounces--unless embedded with love in the human heart.

Until I was 3 I lived across the street from Athletic Field in Billings, Montana, home to the Mustangs. Evenings my brother and I would rush across the street through the cooling air to the chain link fence encircling the field. Twining our small fingers in the links, our noses pressed against the cool wire, we watched batting practice, shivering with delight, watching white balls soar into the blue sky.

Those memories laid the rails the train of my life has driven on ever since.

One day as we were sitting on our lawn facing deserted Athletic Field hearing thumps and clacks of cleaning crews bouncing around the empty seats, as though seeking something lost, my father smiled at me, hiding something behind his back.

"Which hand?" he asked. I pointed. He showed me a baseball. "Here, catch," he said, under-handing it. I missed it. He retrieved it. "Ready? Here, catch." I did. "Yaay!" he said.

I clutched the ball tightly against my chest, running my thumb over the raised red stitches where a tiny chicken with red ink on its feet had raced around the ball. "Pretty," I said, "Pretty."

"Yes, pretty," he said. He ruffled my hair. He had tears in his eyes. I didn't know that that was the day my father was going to leave us, as Mom had divorced him.

From then on baseball consumed me. When I was 13 we built Woehl Stadium in the little North Dakota town where our fatherless family had moved, and played every chance we got.

Ten years after that the great wheel of life came full circle when my brother Ron beckoned me out of the stands at an

American Legion baseball game in Jamestown. I remained unaware of the imminent whirring alignment of my stars. The crack of the balls in batting practice, the sounds, smells, the chain link fence all reminded me of those early baseball days in Billing. And my father, absent now twenty years.

Ron jolted me out of my reverie. "C'mon," he said. "Somebody I want you to meet."

"What? Who?"

"A surprise." His eyes were dancing.

Grudgingly I trudged across a green sward of grass toward the chain-link fence enclosing the playing area, where a boy perhaps 16 stood with "Williston" emblazoned in large red letters on his uniform. He looked vaguely familiar.

He clutched a baseball glove and a white baseball with red seams. He nodded to Ron and smiled at me and cocked his head and underhanded the ball to me. "Here, catch," he said.

My eyes widened. Pictures flashed in my mind, the lawn, my father, that last day. Then a wild rush of pent-up emotion, of understanding. A gong reverberated in my skull. Suddenly I was gasping.

I nearly dropped the ball when Ron said, "Bill, this is your brother Jim. Jim, your brother Bill."

Open-mouthed, we stared at each other. Then slowly reached across the chain link fence and shook, then clasped, hands. Familiar face. Dead ringer for my father 20 years earlier.

I blew out my breath. What do you say the first time you meet your previously-unknown 16-year-old half-sibling?

"So," I said inanely, "Baseball?"

He smiled shyly, nodding. "Dad--our dad, I guess, played catch with me on the lawn all the time. Until he left." His eyes drifted. He shrugged. "I love the game, but it's, a, it reminds me of him, I guess."

I nodded. Exactly what I'd been thinking. My loss--and now his loss--but both of our gains as well.

We shook again. In a daze I drifted back to my seat. After that I learned of him through game statistics in the sports pages, and saw him at various sporting events, and at times when he refereed games I played in. But never again connected with him.

A Big Sports Venture

In 1978, I was big into sports, playing amateur basketball, baseball, slow-pitch softball, coaching, running seven miles a day for the fun of it, and following sports in general. So why not start a sports magazine? I planned big, a *Sports Illustrated* for North Dakota, tabloid newspaper size, with black and white photos, covering every aspect of the state's sports. An early *North Dakota Sports Journal's* writing contest winner wrote about rodeo.

Looking back, I must have been half-crazed to try the idea, producing *The Journal* of 16 pages--four full newspaper sheets--in nine-point type every two weeks, averaging 30,000 words an issue--that's half the size of an Agatha Christie mystery novel. I created all the ideas, and wrote three-quarters of the pieces, "On Sports Injuries," (knees, Achilles tendons), game predictions ("The Mad Prognosticator"), and running ("I want to be out in the hills, the blue bowl of the sky above me, the birds flitting around me, the ground disappearing beneath my running feet," said one of my entries).

Each issue contained something for everybody--interviews with high school boy and girl coaches, and players. I even interviewed New York Knick Phil Jackson, who said, "When I was young I wanted to win so badly I cried after losing a championship game in the seventh grade. I dislike losing intensely. I would have liked to play baseball professionally, but the seasons are too long, and basketball was a sure thing."

Other *NDSJ* included columns like "What Sports Has Done for Me," Fellowship of Christian Athletes, gym sizes, and trivia contests, like off who did Babe Ruth hit his called-shot home run? Charley Root. (Ruth said, "If I'd have missed it, I'd have looked like an awful fool.") Also biorhythms, fiction, quotes, word games.

My friend Jim Clark thought the project was a great idea, and was kind enough to drive 70 miles from Bismarck the night before the first paper was due at the printer to help me set it together. I had all the copy typed, so we cut and pasted and added headlines. I gave out about 3 AM, having to teach at Fort Yates the next day. But stalwart Jim worked through the night, and finished it by 7 AM as I rose. He also came down other times to help.

I had 1,000 copies printed. Jim and I handed them out at the well-attended State Class B boys' high school basketball tournament in Bismarck, figuring attendees would read the paper, let others know how wonderful it was, and subscribe.

Yet after each tournament game I was disappointed to see tons of the papers strewn about with order blanks still intact.

But I still had hope. Having previously owned two bookstores, I had an in with distributor Saks News of Bismarck, who placed copies on newsstands across the state.

After returns for the first issue came in, I was ecstatic. Every one had sold! 1,000! Unbelievable! All that work had paid off in the form of success--and a large check.

But a week later reality set in. Saks needed me to return the check--they'd mistakenly paid me for every copy, not the 50 that actually sold. The handwriting was on the wall, though I didn't heed it yet. But eventually the hard work caught up to me. After seven issues in four months, I refunded subscriber their remaining monies, and stopped publishing.

Though the venture might sound like a failure, I didn't view it that way. I learned that things don't always go as you want them to go; I learned how to interview, the staple of my 40-year-writing career. I learned how to produce many ideas and prose under pressure in a short time; and most of all, I learned the gift of true friendship from Jim.

One Perfect Baseball Summer

Each spring we grunted our push mowers into the knee-high grass of the empty lot three blocks from home. The reels clogged often, but we didn't care. When they whirred free we were slicing down the outfield grass of the baseball stadium we had built, a place to play until the New York Yankees called.

We sheared the outfield, straightened out or added bases if they'd gone missing during the winter, fixed the pitcher's mound, made sure the backstop was solid, and spruced up the dugout, an old wood-reinforced Kelvinator box. And now the *coup de grace*, a correctly-sized wooden home plate made in shop class.

Finished, sweaty, exhausted, jubilant, and a bit awed, we admired the stadium's sleek lines. We named it Woehl Stadium after my uncle who owned the land.

"Play ball!" we screamed, sprinting to home to choose sides.

Often that summer up to 10 of us, 13-14 years old, raced to the Stadium to play baseball every chance we got. We kept batting statistics, and marked monumental home runs with Popsicle sticks stuck into the ground in the Gutschmidts' garden across the street.

Our members included Ergy Burp (a nickname Ervin detested) 39 years old, who was, his parents said, "Not right," after falling off a hay rack at thirteen and striking his temple on the sharp edge. We teased Ervin about his engineer's cap and his ancient mitt, stiff as a five-fingered board, and whooped at his crazy swing, like he was smacking a fence post straight down into the ground.

When I was on the mound he retaliated with, "Heyyy, Biddee! We want a pitcher, not a glass of water, hee hee hee!"

One day Ervin and I became inextricably yoked together. He wound up like pitchers of yore, pumping his arms up and down before he fired a fastball to me at the plate.

The mound was only 30 feet away. I swung the nailed-together electrical-tape-wrapped bat and smacked the ball on the sweet spot. Crack! I rocketed a scalding line drive back at Ervin. He couldn't react. He didn't move as it whacked him solidly--in the crotch.

He dropped like a sack of potatoes and lay unmoving. I killed him! I thought. I jumped on him and thumped his chest. "Ervin!" I cried, "Ervin!" I looked up. "God, please let him live and I'll never call him Ergy Burp again!"

Slowly his eyes opened. They were distant, then focused on me. He smiled painfully, and said, "Oooh Biddy, you hit that one good, hee hee hee."

After that perfect summer, life changed. Chores and jobs and girls called players away. We played less, then not at all. The years drifted away.

Each time I came home, if I saw Ervin he covered his crotch and said, "Oooh Biddy, you hit that one good, hee hee hee."

Many years later, I returned to old Woehl Stadium, weed-infested, all our efforts crumbled into nothing.

Flooded with memories, I poked in the weeds for second base, the pitcher's mound, home plate. I heard rustling behind me, and an angry voice cried, "Heyyyy! You get out of here. Right now!"

I turned, and a stooped old man with white hair, wearing an engineer's cap, strode towards me, glaring. He brandished a bat, and held a ball in his stiff mitt.

For a moment I was taken aback. Then I said, "Ervin! It's me. Bill!"

He stopped. His rheumy eyes went wide, and a great smile creased his lined face. "Biddy!" he choked, "Biddy!" He covered his crotch and said, "Oooh Biddy, you hit that one good, hee hee hee."

We underhanded the ball back and forth, reminiscing, until he grabbed the bat and stood at the plate. "Heyyy! We want a pitcher," he said, "hee hee, not a glass of water."

I wound up and tossed him a soft pitch. It took him a few to match his swing to my lobs.

Then, crack! The ball sailed over my head, just far enough for us to glory in its arc. And that perfect baseball summer.

Often these days when I hear the crack of a bat, I will remember those glorious days of youth paying baseball at Woehl Stadium--and Ervin.

Ervin loved to play baseball whenever we wanted to.

Proof of Ancient Peoples

I never got to dig in an actual ancient site until the Oahe Dam in South Dakota was finished in 1959, and the backing-up waters began to inundate old Indian sites on the banks of the Missouri River in North Dakota, eventually forcing archaeologists to perform incomplete excavating because of the sheer number of sites that required work simultaneously before they were covered by water.

My brother Ron had worked on one of those archaeological sites one summer, so when the work on it was finished, and it was abandoned, we checked that site to see what we could find.

I began my search along a log half in the water. Moments later, dimly visible in the mud, I spotted a perfectly-honed flint arrowhead about two inches long. My vision went black for an instead, as it had happened before when I get too excited. Seconds later my vision cleared, I reached down and grabbed the arrowhead.

I was overwhelmed by its beauty, and haunted by holding a deadly weapon fashioned from a chip of rock. The piece of flint was probably from the Knife River flint quarry in North Dakota, where Indian tribes from all over the U.S. obtained flint for their weapons for 11,000 years.

I cleaned the arrowhead, and flicked the edge with my thumb, as sharp today as when it had been chipped hundreds of years ago. To the warrior who fashioned it, the arrowhead was a tool, yet its beautiful symmetry made it a work of art.

Ron asked where I had found the arrowhead. He said he'd found a very rare, complete pot in the same area, and took it down to the river to clean it. The pot was muddy, and slippery, and as he washed it, in his excitement the pot slipped out of his hands onto the log, breaking into dozens of pieces.

Later amidst a series of flint chips in one small area, I could imagine a warrior squatting here, deer hide protecting his hand as he pressed the sharp end of an antler tine to knap off chips until it was finished. Did he hold it up to the light and admire its beauty?

We found pottery sherds with different designs, and two small cobs of maize, half the size and length of an index finger.

Examining each of these ancient artifacts flung me back into the past and gave me a small sense of what the people's lives had been like hundreds of years ago.

I found many arrowheads in the empty lot across the street from our house. This arrowhead belongs to Mike Trekell.

Fossils

My second-most successful foray into finding fossils remains embedded only in the deep layers of my memory. It came about in my 20s when a farmer, digging a stock pond in his pasture, scooped up great gulps of earth with a backhoe, and, when six feet down, smelled oil. He had unearthed a cache of fossil fish on a shale shelf.

Ever since finding fossils in the ravine across the street from where I grew up, they have excited me. They raise hordes of questions: what animals are they? How did they die? When? What was the landscape like at the time? The weather? So many questions.

As soon as the university archaeological department finished with the farmer's site, I rushed over. From a hundred feet away I could smell the oil. I climbed the dirt mound, and gazed into the pit at the dozens of fish arrayed across a five-foot-square shale shelf.

I was stunned into muteness. After a moment I roused myself and clambered down into the hole. A dozen fish up to the size of my hand appeared to be swimming in a primordial sea. It was like viewing an aquarium lying on its side. Some fish possessed wisps of color, something I had never experienced before with fossils.

Gingerly I touched several fish, wondering how the archaeologists could abandon all this glory. Was I crashing their active dig?

But I'd been told the archaeologists were finished with the site. So I shrugged, and began to cut into the soft shale and, with a cracking sucking sound, pulled loose a foot-square chunk containing several fish. That uncovered another, even more magnificent, layer of fish--a cornucopia of iridescent, seemingly living, breathing, swimming fish.

I saw them in my mind's eye, viewing these iridescent fish shimmering in vibrant colors as though they had just laid down for a nap. As I exposed more of the layer, I saw fish with red dorsal fins, yellow or blue stripes, colored lips, painted dots. Mind-boggling!

In the process of cutting out these colorful specimens, I left fingerprints behind, wondering if some future archaeologist would see them and be curious about who had been here.

Nauseated by the oily smell, I took my blocks of soft shale and headed home. I could always return for more later.

At home I spread them on my bureau and table, thunderstruck by their beauty. I would have to wait to study them after my weekend softball tournament.

When I returned from the tournament, I flicked on the light--and was greeted with a terrible sight. The fish had dried into the color of fossils--unattractive gray. Almost no color remained. I was heartbroken.

The next day on the way back to the fossil site I planned how to preserve them, with spray lacquer.

I trekked across the pasture, skirting a few grazing Herefords that lifted their heads and gazed at me, as though to say, "You again?" I climbed the mound of dirt. At the top, I stopped and looked down. And almost tumbled down the slope.

The stock pond was filled to the brim with water.

And why not? It was, after all, a stock pond, not the personal stockpile of an amateur archaeologist.

I've never made a comparable discovery since.

This is like those I discovered.
(Wikipedia Creative Commons
Attributions ShareAlike 4.0 License.)

Number of Socks

By the time I ended my running career, I owned 150 pairs of white cotton socks, each set numbered consecutively with a black magic marker on the side of the toe area in large numerals. Though "pairs" might be stretching it, as the thieving sock dragon stole a few half-pairs, and my roommates "borrowed" some. After a proper period of mourning I replaced the missing socks with a new white one with the correct number, so they weren't technically pairs, one old, the other bright white. Plus the colored stripes seldom matched.

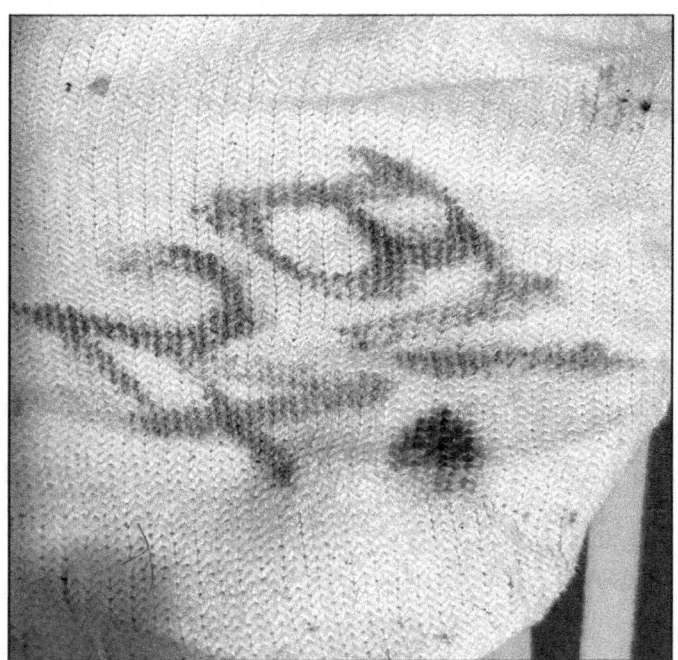

This is the lone numbered sock left out of the original 150 or so.

You might wonder why I did this. For survival. I lived with seven male roommates who played sports or jogged and routinely confiscated my socks until they finished their monthly washings. So often I had no clean socks left, or no socks at all. Hiding them was useless, with eight people packed into two rooms and a bathroom.

Thus buying socks by the truckload allowed me to dig out pairs when I wanted to run my daily seven miles, to glory in nature and gain runner's nirvana. The numbered socks had another advantage: they helped me meet people, like one time when I ran a half-marathon in Grand Forks.

I was single, and as we lined up, I spotted a particular dark-haired beauty, and figured I might as well run with her. I said "Hi," but she just nodded. When the starting gun went off, she already had a bevy of admirers. And I soon realized she ran slower than I did, which would goof up my running rhythm, the body's best and smoothest way of running, which each serious runner discovered after jogging many miles. Altering my rhythm resulted in more effort, so I forgot about her and ran my usual pace, and was feeling good for the second six-and-a-half mile jaunt back. Then I discovered we would be running into the wind.

Not good; ideal running says you run into the wind on the way out, so the running will be easier on the way back when you are tiring. No choice, though. As the fair young maiden came toward me heading to her turn-around, I tried to catch her eye, without success.

Now with the wind working against me, as my rhythm disappeared, and running farther than ever before, I was tiring badly. "Five more to go? Four? Dang!" As I neared the three-mile sign, I blew out a big breath and decided to hang it up.

I slowed and sat down at the side of the road, and removed my running shoes, rubbing my toes. "Ten is enough," I blurted.

A woman's voice behind me said, "No, it's not. You started this race to finish it. Only three more to go. You can do it."

And there she was. "Come on," she said. "We'll run together the rest of the way. You can do it."

Suddenly I felt a surge of energy. I replaced my socks and shoes, and ran. We chatted as we ran, and exchanged first names. Lucky me! I couldn't wait to fall into her arms at the finish line.

"You must run a lot," she said. I smiled, believing she was referring to my sleek form, but she added, "Judging by your numbered socks. You really have, what, one sock says 90, the other 91, that many pair?"

"Well, yes," I said. So I told her the sock story.

She said, "I just had to talk to the person who numbered their socks and find out why," she laughed.

As we neared the end, she sped up and crossed the line ahead of me, where she fell into someone's arms all right--her boyfriend's. Ah well, she did help me finish the only half-marathon I ever ran.

If not for surgeries and the ravages of time, I would still be running today, adding to the 50,000 miles I accumulated over the years, enough to circumnavigate the world twice. Running gained me friends and camaraderie, communion with nature, and every day allowed me to achieve a state of nirvana, the runner's high.

Outsiders in a Strange Land

Living in a new culture means you will stumble into unfamiliar territory that will test your resolve, because you are a stranger in a strange land. Before the car accident, I hadn't thought much about being a non-Indian, *wasicu*, or white man, on an Indian reservation. Other than being mildly irked by it, remindful of being singled out in baseball and softball as a lefthander--"southpaw, sidewinder, lefty"--being a non-Indian had no real effect on me. Yes, my students occasionally let me know in anger or teasing that I was a *wasicu*. Usually not serious. Kids being kids.

Until driving north on N.D. State Highway 1806 in the Standing Rock Sioux Indian Reservation one afternoon. On the car racing toward us I saw the front end dip as the driver hit his brakes and began to turn. He didn't notice us because the low blinding sun shone behind us and into his eyes. My driver, my girlfriend Kathy was angry with me, was speeding, and didn't see the driver start to turn.

At the last second she saw him and swerved. Too late. We smashed into the other car at highway speed. Like a death knell the tremendous crash and screeching of metal filled my ears. The fronts of the cars leaped upward. I was launched toward the windshield, striking my elbow on the dash. Only lap belts in a 1973 AMC Gremlin. I was wearing mine. Kathy was not.

The following silence, except for hissing radiators, was curiously deafening. Smoke rose gently between the vehicles into the late afternoon air.

Kathy seemed okay, as she was moaning, "Oh, my beautiful car, my beautiful car." It was only a year old.

So I hopped out to check on the other driver, already out.

"You all right?" we said simultaneously.

We both nodded.

"Thank God," he said. "The sun..."

After exchanging insurance information, and our engine started, I pried the crushed fender away from the tire, my elbow screaming, and we wobbled back toward Fort Yates. Then I noticed the bowl-sized outdent in the windshield from Kathy's head, and that she was becoming incoherent. But she refused to let me drive.

At the hospital the nurses whisked her back, while I complained about my right elbow. The orderly said, "She's Cherokee," which I knew. "What's your affiliation?"

"Non-Indian," I said.

He shook his head. "I'm sorry. We can't serve non-Indians."

"But what about my elbow?" I said angrily.

"Can you move it? See, not broken. You'll be okay."

Kathy was admitted with a concussion. I went home. Dazed, in my bed, the accident kept repeating over and over again. Hours later I finally dropped off.

I woke up feeling as if I'd gone 10 rounds with Mohammed Ali. But I'd calmed down, and realized that if I had been hurt badly, they would have served me--most Lakota I knew were kind, generous, and helpful; I also thought, why get angry if Ford dealers don't sell new Chevrolets? The reservation was for the Lakota, not the *wasicu*. I was an interloper, an outsider. The tribal hospital didn't have the resources to help everyone--9,500 Lakota and 9,700 non-Indians. Had never been meant to. No rancor there; just the way it was designed.

Shards of the accident and its aftermath popped into my consciousness at random times for weeks afterwards, and made me think more about times I had been an outsider. Like in third grade where all the right-handers got hand supports to help them write. My teacher said, "You're a lefthander, but yours will come next week." Which of course it didn't.

Everyone feels like an outsider at one time or another. Most are temporary.

From that thought it wasn't a long jump to thinking about my forebears who had once been outsiders--strangers in a strange land--my Germans-from-the-Ukraine grandfathers, who emigrated, bereft of English. Like most immigrants, they were at first non-Americans. But they persevered, fulfilling their great dreams of owning their own land--to farm, and enjoy the freedom that went with it. Until one day when they were no longer outsiders, but Americans, in their own country.

So I owe them debt of gratitude, for without them, I obviously would never have had the life-altering experience of teaching on the reservation--even if for a while I became a stranger in a strange land.

A Hairy Situation

Growing up in a Germans-from-the-Ukraine community, the melding of English with ancient German in normal speaking was usual: as my mother said, "Whichever word in whichever language comes out easiest."

After hearing all that mixing, I assumed other dual-language cultures spoke the same way. So when I started teaching on the Standing Rock Sioux Indian Reservation in North Dakota, I expected to hear that same kind of language mix in the hallways and classrooms, English intermingled with Dakota or Lakota or Nakota.

But I didn't. I wondered if it was happening but I had missed it, engrossed as I was in teaching new classes in a new-to-me culture in a new school in a new community while attempting to learn the names of 150 new students.

But after paying close attention, I didn't hear any "foreign" words until one day while walking in the aisle of a grade seven classroom, and commenting on that day's lesson. Suddenly the hand of a girl shot out and grabbed my wrist. With her other hand she began rubbing her fingers back and forth through the hair on my arm. I was surprised, but didn't feel threatened, so I allowed her to continue rubbing.

"*Shunka!*" she said in a low voice, "*Shunka.*"

Her friend moaned in shock. "Claudia!" she said. "Claudia!"

Claudia clunked her head down on her desk, embarrassed. Other kids in the class gazed at her with wide eyes, mouths agape.

Seeing that Claudia was feeling bad, I decided not to make a big deal out of the situation. But after class I asked my Lakota aide, Jeannette, what "*Shunka*" meant.

She looked uncertain, and said she shouldn't tell me. Made me even more curious. "Now you have to tell me," I said.

"You really want to know?"

I nodded.

She took a deep breath and said, "Well, first I have to say the kids have a nickname for you. They call you '*E-day-ish-ma*.'"

"And what does *E-day-ish-ma* mean?"

She smiled uncertainly. "Well, um, the hairy one."

Now I had to smile. I possessed a full black beard and mustache, and hairy arms, so the nickname seemed warranted. I shrugged. "How about '*Shunka*'?"

She seemed embarrassed. "*Shunka* means 'Dog.'"

I blinked. At that I wasn't sure what to think. That's when I realized that most Lakota men had little and light body hair, so I doubtless was an anomaly to Claudia.

For a week that class returned to normal until a trio of girls loitered around my desk as class ended. The kids loved to play tricks on teachers, hiding the stapler, unplugging the wall clock, or dropping my pens on the floor--when I wasn't noticing. The girls seemed nervous. "What can I help you with?" I asked, noting the stapler, clock, and pens were okay.

When the room was empty except for those three, one of the girls hemmed and hawed and asked to touch my beard.

"Sure," I shrugged. Why not? So she did, and emitted a little scream.

The second girl touched my beard and nodded, saying, "Claudia's right, *Shunka*."

The third girl felt my beard and said, "No, *Shunka-khan*."

They left, giggling. I asked Jeanette about the last word. She smiled. "*Shunka-khan* means 'big dog,' – or 'horse.'"

I was amazed at their courage. Maybe those events made that class the most receptive and easiest to discipline.

During my two-year stay I never heard a mixture of words in sentences as at home, but did learn a few more words, like *wicasa* (man) *Winyan* (woman) and most common, *wasicu* (vah-sheet-shu) meaning white man, white person, or non-Indian--along with others.

But none ever resonated like *e-day-ish-ma,* the "hairy one."

The Saga of Alfred

During the latter part of October each year, my mind turns back to the door banging open on my grade seven classroom at Fort Yates, North Dakota, on the Standing Rock Sioux Indian Reservation. A small bundle of a kid was tossed in like a sack of potatoes. He skidded, sprawling out on the carpet. The truant officer jabbed a finger at the boy. "That's a bad one," he said. "You've got to watch him," he said of the slowly unwinding pile of humanity on the floor. "He's a Has Horns, a bad one," he said again as he stepped outside and slammed the door.

After the class settled down, and I had a free moment, I knelt beside Alfred's desk and asked him what was going on.

He smiled and a light came on in his eyes. He waved his hands airily. "Those guys," he said, "no comp."

No comp--"no competition," meant the probation officers were no competition in catching him. When school was about to start, Alfred had saddled up his horse, packed foodstuffs in his saddlebags, water, and whatever else he needed to survive. When he spotted the parole officers barreling down the dusty road to his house, he hopped aboard his horse and rode out into the wild hills, where automobiles couldn't follow.

"They couldn't catch me," he said, waving his hand again. "No comp."

"But Alfred," I said. "You're here in school now. If they were no comp, how did they catch you?"

He got a sheepish grin and then laughed. "Getting kinda cold out there at night now," he said. "So I let them catch me."

For the most part, Alfred was a quiet if unstudious student. One day a firecracker blew up during the middle of the spelling test, sending everyone out of their desks, shrieking and yelling.

Except Alfred. While hundreds of fragments of firecracker paper drifted in the sunbeams, he sat, his face near his paper, writing, his little pink tongue sticking out of the side of his mouth.

"Alfred," I said, "why did you light that firecracker?"

Dreamily, he looked up at me. "What firecracker?" he said. I could only laugh.

For the most part, Alfred, a full-blooded Hunkpapa Sioux, was not a problem. If I pushed him too hard, he'd look at me, and say, "*Wasicu* (white man), remember that it was my people who killed yellow-hair (Custer.)" Basically, "Back off."

He muddled through the rest of the year, but failed.

Early the next school year, I stepped into my eighth-grade Language Arts classroom, and there in the front row, sitting close to my desk, sat Alfred, Smiling, grinning. I explained he would have to redo grade seven L.A.

A week later, he disappeared. Later I found he had transferred to Kenel, South Dakota, another reservation school, and enrolled--as an eighth-grader.

And failed. Because so many reservation kids transferred willy-nilly in those days, their paperwork was slow to follow. One year I had a transfer into my class on the last day of school.

The next year I went into writing, and perhaps halfway through the school year, went to visit teacher-friends in Fort Yates. I had also taught ninth-grade, so I was walking through the high school halls when I heard a locker door slam. I turned, and there was Alfred. When he saw me, a big grin spread on his face.

"Alfred," I said, "what are you doing here?"

He put his finger to his lips and said, "Shh! This year I'm a sophomore!"

From the time I spent teaching on the Reservation, I will always cherish two things out of many: the evocative and beautiful last names: Kills Pretty Enemy, Swift Horse, Has Horns, Little Horse, Holy Elk Face, Left Hand--and Alfred. And realized that sometimes some of your students could take your heart with them.

The Cat's Meow

We were not trying to torture my poor cat. Or ourselves. Honest. We were merely attempting to transfer my furry friend 393 miles from North Dakota to my new home in Minnesota. In a fully-packed Chevette. Without air conditioning. With the temperature--outside and inside--approaching a hundred.

I had read that slathering butter on the back of a cat's paws would keep her occupied on a long trip. I also figured a private cardboard apartment with flaps closed would offer her solitude, coziness, and keep her out of our hair.

A few miles down the road, yowling and scrabbling, Mittens poked her head up through the flaps, glaring at me, a disembodied cat head setting atop a box. She catapulted out and raced back and forth, clawing my shirts, smearing butter on them with each pass.

Rugby's uptown was jammed with Crazy Days cars and revelers. As I got out, Mittens escaped, bounding joyfully down the sidewalk, playing tag with us, racing under car after car, tail held high, as though to say, "Ha! Can't catch me!"

She disappeared under and up into the engine compartment of a big Oldsmobile 88, safe from her tormentors. The owner happened to be nearby, and we begged him to pop the hood, revealing Mittens, hot and miserable, and got her out.

In the library's lawn sprinkler a block away, I held her upside down by all fours, trying to cool her belly, sopping both of us with cold water, while she wailed bloody murder. Passersby fixed me with the evil eye. "That poor cat," someone muttered.

Merely the beginning of our travails; only 380 miles to go.

Disembarking at Nikki's sister's house in Devils Lake, a huge feral cat scared her. Growling, Mittens got loose, and disappeared into a culvert.

Lying on my stomach in the hot sand, I could see her eyes glinting in the dim light inside the culvert. She gazed contentedly at me as though to say, "Nice and cool in here, thank you."

I spoke gently and pushed my arm in slowly, hoping to grab her. As though she knew the exact length of my reach--"Let's see, he's an eight, so right here should be perfect,"--I could barely touch her cold nose.

She licked my finger twice, as though saying, "No hard feelings, mate. I still like you. But it's comfortable in here, and I'll come out when I'm ready."

Twenty minutes later a can of her favorite cat food outside the entrance finally lured her out. 310 miles to go.

On the road again, we placed a plastic bag of ice cubes on her panting tummy while she hid deep under the front seat.

Nikki had always wanted to see a missile silo, so 30 miles further east we turned into one, and stopped.

Diabolical Mittens scratched Nikki and escaped again, shooting through a small opening in the chain-link fence right into the missile complex. She found a comfortable spot in the shade of the monstrous concrete missile cap, circled a couple of times, and lay down.

Uh oh, I thought, noting the signs on the fence for the first time: **Warning: Restricted Area. Unlawful to enter.** Double uh oh. And in vivid blood-red: **Use of deadly force authorized.**

Yikes! Clearly the only way in was over the concertina wire at the top which neither of us was going to try. We waited, nervously glancing up into the blue sky, anticipating a missile screaming down any minute, or a convoy of Air Force vehicles screeching to a halt, cuffing us and taking us away while Mittens said, "Free at last!"

Eventually Mittens sauntered out, looking like, "I'm ready. How about you guys?"

Who knows how a cat thinks? We drove the final 280 miles without another incident. In our new home she lived with us for 20 more years, a daily gift of joy and fun for us and friends, before passing on ten years ago, leaving us with a spate of good memories.

Remembering Tom

Many of us have a season of sadness, and mine falls in winter, January, when I miss my friend Tom the most. He was a fellow teacher who shared living space with Larry and me for a year. He was also one of the most unique people I've ever known. Sometimes we rolled our eyes, like one morning when he stepped out of the bathroom with towels draped over his arm like a maitre d'.

"How many people live in this trailer?" he said.

Larry and I looked at each other, and said, "Three."

"Well then," he said, "why are there four towels out?"

If a pencil, sock, book, or anything lay on the floor, dropped accidentally by one of us, Tom would stop in front of it, raise one knee high, like a majorette, and step over it with feet to spare.

To illustrate the immensity of our solar system, he designated the school's science room at the west edge of our village as the sun. Heading east into town, different buildings and houses were designated Mercury, Venus, Earth, Mars, and so on, finishing with Pluto at the crossroads two miles out.

Originally from Ohio, Tom misunderstood snow. One time the white stuff was piled 10 feet high around the perimeter of our trailer court by plows, with an ample opening for cars to pass through. Tom revved his car engine until it screamed, and shot full speed backwards. Whammo! Driving the rear end deep into the snow bank. With difficulty Larry and I shoveled him out. Only to see him try again, plunging his car deep into the snow pile once more. He muttered that snow was harder than he thought.

Any loud music except opera troubled Tom. Several times in a café, if a pop song came on the radio while he ate, Tom fled.

Once he spotted a sign that read, "Candy bars .50 cents each." Which, of course, meant half a cent, when they'd meant 50 cents, not ½ cent. Tom bought a Snickers, dropped a penny on the counter, and said, "Keep the change."

Whenever he finished a can of pop, he threw his head back and balanced the can on his lips until the last drop dripped down into his mouth.

His memory was phenomenal, his store of jokes unending. If I didn't laugh at the joke he'd frown and say, "That's strange. It was funny in *Dial* magazine in June 1942."

He knew in excruciating detail everything about every movie, because as a kid he'd watched three to six double features every weekend, six to 12 movies. Name one and he'd recite year, cast, director, story, if a remake, he'd compare the two movies, and the different actors and actresses, and awards, if any.

Every month before he drove up to Winnipeg, he took orders from townspeople for Chinese food, absent in our area, writing the info in a tiny shirt-pocket-size spiral-bound notebook.

At least I assumed it was written. Until I saw the notebook. Everything was typed. "How in the world did you do that?" I asked, trying to figure how he rolled the tiny notebook into his typewriter.

No. He unscrewed the spiral wire, removed a sheet, typed the orders front and back, reassembled the pages, and screwed the wire back in. Upon delivery, he accepted only the exact cost.

He loved to quiz me. "Name the five smallest countries in Europe. What were the previous names of five African nations? What books did John Steinbeck write?" He'd tick them off on his fingers as I tried to answer.

Tom's great wound emanated from his fiance overthrowing him in 1949. After that, he never dated. "When you've had perfection," he sighed, "chances of finding another person so perfect are zero."

One day when the world was too much with him, Tom Parent sent his obituary to the local newspaper, and then sat in his car in a closed garage and left the vehicle running.

When a friend decamps the world by his own hand, the shock and sadness make you wonder, what could I have done differently? When the long sharp knives of life slice a person into shreds inside, you realize stopping him probably wasn't possible.

Experiencing Caribbean Culture

Every other evening Herman the breadman plodded through our campground like an outdoor waiter, bearing on his thin shoulder a huge wooden tray three inches high, piled with small loaves of warm bread under a white cloth. He offered wheat bread, banana bread, and coconut bread. The last two were understandable, considering this small tent encampment near Brewer's Bay, Tortola, British Virgin Islands.

Herman asked only $1.50 per loaf, and before he handed it to us--and there were many of us--he wrapped it in aluminum foil. When I asked for three loaves, Herman said, "That will be one dollar and one dollar and one dollar, three dollars, or something like that." We all chuckled as I handed over a five and told him to keep the change.

Herman the breadman offered nice warm bread for $1.50 a loaf.

Herman was a fount of local information, answering questions about when Styles' taxi might come again, what geckos ate (each other, among other foods) while crying "Warm bread! Warm bread!" From him I first heard about the voodoo dolls.

This was the life, an extra week in the warm tropical sun developing writing ideas while my compatriots, teachers and students, had had to fly home after bare-boating for a week in the warm waters around the islands.

One day I helped an acquaintance row out half a mile into the bay, lowering microphones to listen to moaning whales; on another day I struggled down a long rocky trail to a cache of ancient petroglyphs while geckos scuttled into the rustling dead leaves.

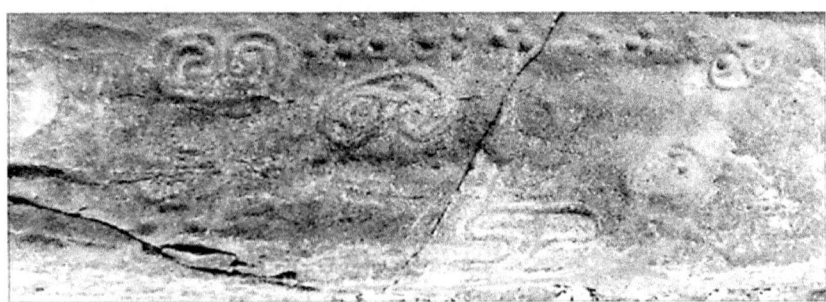

Who made the BVI petroglyphs is uncertain: they could be done by early island Indians, or of African origin.

Without electricity, evenings groups of us campers gathered around a crackling fire eating delectable communal fish and chunks of banana bread or coconut bread slathered with butter and jam. We solved the world's problems while playing scrabble, or cards, or reading, in the flickering firelight. A true paradise.

Each night I slipped into my sleeping bag amidst the utter darkness, listening to the rustle of the banana leaves and palm fronds in the gentle wind above, while the Caribbean waters hissed onto the beach 50 yards away.

Europeans first discovered the islands of the Arawaks, in 1493, during Columbus' second voyage. He named the islands *Santa Ursula y las Once Mil Vírgenes,* or Saint Ursula and her 11,000 Virgins. Today they are called "The Virgins", "British" or "American."

They, like all Caribbean Islands, are another world in many ways, including some beliefs in the dark arts. One evening a woman produced a voodoo doll--a skull of a hollowed-out, dried coconut with holes for eyes and nose, and an open slash for a mouth. It reminded me of shrunken skulls--with green hair in the form of palm fronds thrust into a hole in the top.

"Ta da!" she said. "Voodoo if you believe in that rot."

I didn't, but thought a skull like that would be an unusual souvenir to bring back home. If only I knew...

Herman laughed. "You too, mon? Problems with a lost love? A jealous suitor?" He shook his head. "I shall bring the remedy."

After he brought the voodoo doll, I didn't pack it for fear of breaking the drying fronds. In Puerto Rico I laid it on the customs counter as I unfolded my traveling papers.

"Yiiii!" Mr. Customs Agent screamed, leaping backwards. "What is that?"

I shrugged. "A voodoo doll."

"Yiiii!" he said again. "Go go go!" His eyes were huge as he held up his hands as if in surrender. He pointed urgently. "Go! Go!"

So I did. Thus it remains possible that some dusty records somewhere might show that I have never returned from the British Virgin Islands.

At home, the coconut skull was a minor conversation piece with friends. But it never produced such a strong reaction again.

The Singing in the Oceans

A mile out among the gentle swells of the Atlantic Ocean, with a thousand feet of the great deeps beneath us, Paul Knapp cut the engine on his inflatable dinghy. Water lapped against the sides. We sat for a moment, enjoying the amazing silence.

"This should do," he said. With a splash he tossed a basketball-sized rock overboard on a 30-foot rope attached to the dinghy, and to a pair of white buoys to moor us. They bobbed up and down.

I was nervous because I didn't swim well, and wondered what we would do if the rubber boat sprang a leak? Or if a rogue current grabbed us and carried us out into the two thousand miles of water with no land up towards Newfoundland? The ocean was a foot below the gunwale, waiting to climb aboard. A recent big storm had swept in on huge waves and pummeled the beach near my tent into smithereens. Maybe another lurked over the horizon. I also possessed an unreasoning fear that all sharks were searching particularly for Bill Vossler. Plus, nobody knew we were out here.

To stem my nervousness, I peered over my shoulder to glimpse Tortola, the island in the British Virgin chain from where we'd come. There it was, a dark slash on the horizon with green palm trees and a white sand beach. I breathed a sigh of relief.

On that day, we motored out into the trackless gray waters to listen to humpback whales sing. I'd never heard their ministrations called singing before. I knew the great 50 foot-long, 50-ton mammals made sounds, but I'd never paid attention. I thought they were meaningless grunts, like noises made by dogs and frogs and other animals, expressing hunger or pain.

But I was alone in the BVI, looking for something to do, and thought Paul might make an article. He said he'd gotten interested hearing Jacques Cousteau's "The Singing Whale." His interest spiked when he heard that mating songs of the males changed. "I got hooked wanting to hear the new songs."

Male humpbacks are underwater composers, who alter their songs or create new ones to impress different possible mates--an aria here, an oratorio there, in Whalespeak. Maybe even an opera, as songs can last 20 minutes.

Paul dropped his waterproof microphone, or hydrophone, into the sea. "I learned to set it 30 feet down where you get away from the clicking of the pistol shrimp. No deeper is needed."

As the hydrophone slipped into the depths, ocean sounds--drifting in from as far as 10 miles away--emanated from the speakers. Paul named them, a chorus of crackling from pistol shrimp, an engine, lobsters making scratchy sounds with antenna, parrot-fish eating algae off coral. "Once porpoises checked out the microphone with their sonar, clicking and whistling. I just wanted to cry."

I frowned. Nothing to cry about here. Like static from the phonograph needle when a record is over. I thought of putting my notebook away, but didn't want to hurt Paul's feelings.

More static. Paul glanced at his watch. For a moment, nothing. But then--oh then--a deep thrilling moan grabbed me and shook me. It rose and fell, morphing into groaning, wailing, crying, a cacophony of songs nearly indescribable, yet incandescent, so alien yet gorgeous that the hair stood on the back of my neck.

The trickling sound of deep water had me believing I was in the water next to the beasts as their voices ranged from deep bass to soprano, an incredible range, vibrato, grunts, sound after sound after sound. Paul said in a low voice, as though he was in a place of worship, "Hearing this singing is such a personal thing. It's good for us. We need that singing. It expresses the universal yearning of creatures of and for the earth, of and for my own great yearning."

I could only nod. I leaned closer to the speakers, enraptured by the eerie but lovely overtures.

A half-hour later--or maybe three hours, Paul retrieved the buoys and rock and hydrophone, and we headed back, while I joyed in experiencing another wonder of our marvelous world.

"Mr. Vossler, You Should Be Dead."

One Monday morning a new rounds doctor stepped into my hospital room, riffed through the pages on my clipboard, inhaled sharply, and looked at me.

"Mr. Vossler," she said, wide-eyed. "You should be dead."

A month earlier in June 1994 I was playing softball for a Bethlehem Lutheran church team in St. Cloud, when I slammed the softball over the head of the right fielder. As he pursued it, I circled the bases, thinking of an inside-the-park home run.

Twenty feet from home plate I heard a loud snap and felt a sharp pain in front of my left knee. I staggered a couple of steps, and went down. I crawled toward home plate as the throw came in. I was a few feet away when the catcher caught the ball and tagged me. "You're out!" he said.

The umpire took pity and said, "No he isn't." But that's not the rule, so I was out, as I should be. And out of the game.

I had no idea how that injury would affect my life. I knew about major injuries--I'd torn my Achilles tendon playing basketball, and knew this was major, too, so I understood recovery would be long and grueling.

At the emergency room they said I had a torn patellar tendon and a broken kneecap. Which meant surgery and physical therapy starting the next day.

After returning home from surgery, I worked on the exercises, making progress, but unaware of what lurked inside me.

Five weeks later, I began coughing. As I climbed the stairs from my basement office, I could only take a couple of steps before having to stop, coughing and fighting for breath.

I visited a different doctor as my regular one was on vacation. The substitute determined I had bronchitis. So he prescribed an antibiotic. Which didn't help. I continued to cough, and struggle for breath.

Luckily, I had a physical therapy appointment two days after the doctor's appointment. And doubly luckily, the weather was hot, so I wore shorts.

As I sat on the inflated ball and began doing my exercises, the physical therapy attendant got a good look at my left leg, the thigh bluish and distended. He touched it and found it clammy. He made a noise, and called an ambulance to hustle me to the hospital for an ultrasound. It showed a massive blood clot in my left leg, calf to groin.

Doctors and nurses rushed into action. I was hooked up with monitors and an IV and given pills. Everyone seemed very intense and worried. The medical people had determined that my cough was not bronchitis--but pulmonary embolisms caused by clots that had broken loose from my leg, and lodged in my lungs. Limiting my air supply. If I had been told the possible consequences of the blood clots in my lungs, I would have freaked.

That was left for the Monday morning doctor, telling me, "Mr. Vossler, you should be dead."

"What?" I said, more than stunned.

"A pulmonary embolism untreated as long as yours usually kills the patient."

I was shocked into incoherence. I never realized the danger, and the situation explained the reactions of the medical staff in the hospital.

She said, "You're not out of the woods yet. If more clots break loose while you're being treated…"

Luckily, none did. After a few more tense days, I was sent home, where I learned that more people die each year from pulmonary embolisms than breast cancer, HIV, and auto accidents--combined.

So since that time, how could I not be thankful, and have thanks coursing through my veins with every heartbeat? How could I not renew my thanks every Thanksgiving--as well as every day--for the life I am privileged to continue to lead?

Love of Dinosaurs Never Dies

Some people never outgrow their love of dinosaurs. As long as I can remember, I've loved dinosaurs, especially the basic four of my youth: the monstrous *brontosaurus* of 50,000 pounds, scarfer of hundreds of pounds of leaves each day that they swallowed without chewing; the *triceratops* of huge three-horn fame, called the toughest dinosaur of all; the *stegosaurus*, who for a number of years was thought to have a larger brain in its tail to control its spike at the end, the thagomizer (named by cartoonist Gary Larson in *The Far Side*); and of course, *Tyrannosaurus rex,* king of the tyrant lizards, the dinosaur that everyone recognizes, and fears.

When I was 11 years old and in the beginning throes of my love of affair of the beasts, we moved into a house across the street from an empty lot with a three-foot-deep, water-scoured ravine whose walls revealed ancient artifacts. I was sure they were fossils of dinosaurs, chiefly *T. rex*. With the hot sun beating down, I dug them out of the walls using Mom's silverware (until she stopped me from using them), packaged the fossils up and shipped them to the Smithsonian Institution in Washington, D.C., for identification, which I was astounded to discover they did free of charge.

Not dinosaurs, but from the ice age, remnants from the Pleistocene. Extinct horse, camel, and bison. I exhibited these fossils and the Smithsonian IDs to my classmates. The pieces were at 25,000 years to 100,000 years old. Who else had something like that?

Despite finally accepting that I had not found anything dinosaurian, I was not deterred. I continued hunting for elusive dinosaur bones in the empty lot, and other sites for dinosaur hunting into my adult life.

Two summers ago Nikki and I dug for dinosaurs at Bismarck, where I unearthed a number of amber pellets, and part of a rib of an *Edmontosaurus* dinosaur, while Nikki found the other half of the rib. These 40-foot-long 10-ton plant-eating beasts walked on two legs or four, and were *T. rexes'* favorite lunch.

So, I never outgrew my love of dinosaurs.

The *Edmontosaurus* was one of *T. rex's* favorite foods. (Darius Sankowski, Pixabay.)

The *allosaurus* was the first predator in the Jurassic era. (Parker West, Pixabay.)

Dinosaur Hunting Success

A complete *Tyrannosaurus rex*. That's what I'm going to unearth during my first official dinosaur dig, I figure. Heck, two Tyrannos. Think big.

A spray of gravel pings off the fenders of the Jeep Cherokee I'm riding in, interrupting my thoughts. Glancing out the window I see the bottom of a canyon 150 feet below. The rutted gravel road we're flying over slices some 2 miles into the buttes of northwest Wyoming near Thermopolis--dinosaur country.

Dinosaur bones are usually associated with grayish-green rock called the Morrison Formation. That is found by Thermopolis, an area bone-rich beyond belief, with 50 dinosaur sites identified, 3,000 bones removed, thousands more found and perhaps hundreds of thousands hidden.

"We have so many sites but not enough staff to dig on them all," says Sean Fishbaugh of the Wyoming Dinosaur Center. "So we have our Dig for a Day Program to get help."

Which is why I came to this dinosaur country. And to write for *Compressed Air* magazine, the house organ of Ingersoll Rand Company, which paid me to participate in the Dig for a Day for one day, and afterwards get additionally paid to write a magazine article for them. Nikki and I decide to pay for a second day, as the program allows amateurs like us to dig for dinosaur bones alongside professionals. That chance to find an officially-recognized and certified dinosaur bone has also brought us to Wyoming. We start out at the SI (Something Interesting) site. My *T. rex* skeleton awaits.

Driver Eddie Harris says, "Oh, you'll find bones. Practically everyone in Dig-for-a-Day finds dinosaur bones."

Following orientation we are handed tools: geologist's pick, knife, chisel, hand shovel, and two small paintbrushes. We return to the BB (Bone Bed) site, where staff members are also searching for bones.

I begin by removing two feet of overburden, useless rock atop the grayish green rock of the Morrison formation, the sediment laid down 150 million years ago during the Jurassic period, which contains dinosaur bones.

The sun warms my neck as I attack the rock. My hammer thwacks echo off the juniper and sage-covered buttes surrounding the site as I drive my chisel into seemingly impregnable stone. The chisel creates a hairline crack, next blow a wider one. Each hammer swing jolts my bones up into my shoulder.

With the pointed back of the hammer and a grunt I lever the crack wider until a large chunk breaks loose. Dripping sweat and breathing heavily, I lift the slab and examine its sides for fossils-- trilobites, grass stems, mollusks, anything. While turning the rock, I realize these facets haven't seen daylight in 150 million years. Mind-boggling. I have to stop to think about that. As I move these heavy pieces of rock, I learn why this layer is called burden.

The hammer swings open more rock, dotted by hieroglyphs of ancient plant fossils, black squiggles that charcoal your fingers at the slightest touch. Jurassic plant fossils are ubiquitous at the Thermopolis site, but of poor quality.

"By the end of the day," says Eddie, "we'll all be tired of plant fossils."

For the first couple of hours we drive the staff to distraction, jerking them from their own digging with questions:

"Is this bone?"

"How about this?"

Eventually we discover bone basics: if it rubs off, it's not bone, which is harder than rock and three times as heavy; bone is usually deep orange-red; the inside of fossilized bone exhibits the same honeycomb cell structure as present-day bone.

While my reject pile grows, I find small lumps of coal, and a two-inch long segmented fossilized piece of marsh reed.

Stifling heat builds. I gulp water. At noon we drive back to the SI site and a surprisingly cool tent for lunch. Others ask if we found bone yet. We shake our heads. They quickly say we will.

Sean says people come from all over the world to the site, and are envious, because the SI Site is one of only a handful in the world containing dinosaur tracks and bones. It was also an *allosaurus'* feeding site. My ears perk up. The *allosaurus* is my is my second favorite dinosaur.

After lunch, we head back to the BB site to break more rocks. At 4 PM we stop. I haven't found dinosaur bones, but I'm satisfied with the small fossils I've found--one looks like a long winged moth. Plus I removed enough overburden to discover my *T. Rex* tomorrow.

Day two, I awake stiff and creaky, but feeling like a pro. Yet I'm worried. How can I write about finding dinosaur bones if I don't find any? Eddie assures us we will find dinosaur bones today.

Within a half hour, the dig tenor alters. I guzzled water when I see by Nikki's demeanor that she's found something. Eddie concurs: a five-inch long V-shaped bone from the rib of a *diplodocus* dinosaur. I plant a victory kiss on her lips and rush back to my site.

I break rock, and break rock, and work, and sweat drips off my brow. An hour later, with a grunt I heft yet another chunk of rock looking exactly like the hundreds of other grayish-green rocks I've examined, and clunked onto the growing clunker pile.

But though the same, yet different. I glance down and my knees start shaking. Orange-red rock. A dinosaur bone! Like love, you know when you find it. For an instant, my vision goes black.

In a moment I am transported back to my childhood and my big dream of erecting a *T. rex* skeleton in our basement.

Eddie sees me staring at the grayish green rock before me.

"Find something?" she asks.

Silently I point at the colored lump in the cleft of a seam. Her eyes widen. "Oh yes, yes!," she said. You did find something! Bone!"

Not a *T. rex* bone because this is the wrong era, and wrong layer. But this orange-red lump of rock could be from my second-favorite dinosaur, the teeth-spitting *allosaurus*. You can always dream.

The bone looks like a giant finger, 10 times human size. It is broken, so Eddie superglues the end back on, and begins to painstakingly chisel around the bone.

I am disquieted. I get water. I watch Nikki. I eat a candy bar.

Finally Eddie says "Ah!" and extracts the bone from its 150 million-year-old tomb. It is almost the size of my palm. I accept it gingerly, turning it gently, feeling it, smelling it, caressing it, trying to stem my jubilation. For a second I think of licking it.

During a break we visit the articulated foot site to try to help identifying my bone. My heart thumps, for there it is: a near duplicate of my bone in that foot. But mine is larger, from a different species.

The experts study it. The consensus?

Allosaurus! I have found a piece of one of the most vicious hunters of all time, a 35 foot-long rampaging *allosaurus*. One reference says if not for the *allosaurus*, the Jurassic would have been a dinosaur wonderland.

Later, my bone is numbered BB–229 and recorded. Nikki's too. We are in the books.

The rest of the day is anticlimactic. I feel calm and complete. During these two days I've moved tons of rock, made new friends, and achieved a childhood dream of finding a dinosaur bone. What could be finer?

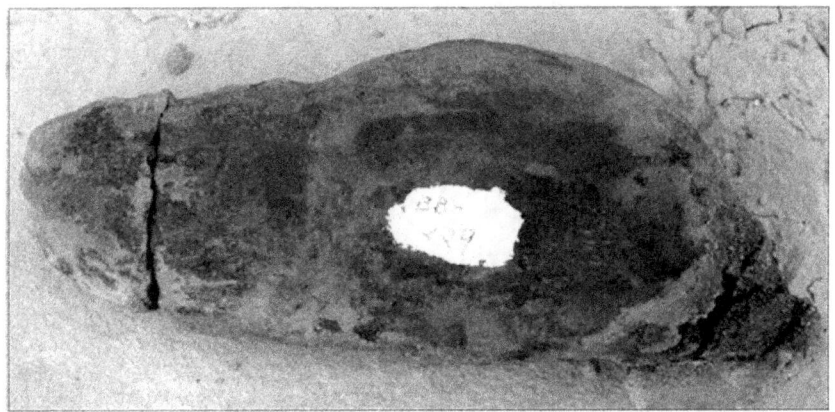

Finding this *allosaurus* finger bone at Thermopolis, Wyoming, met a goal I had had since I was a child: to find a dinosaur bone.

The Morrison Formation above shows heavy formations of rock.

Foggy Foggy Days

Fog has always intrigued me, so the fog discussion in a small back roads cafe on the coast of Nova Scotia intrigued me. First, a wizened man with a leathery face leaned around a post between our tables and said, "Yanks then, eh, by your talk?"

We allowed that we were, and after preliminaries, the discussion drifted to the fog on our ferry-crossing of the Bay of Fundy from Maine, and how beautiful the boats in the harbor looked, bobbing in the mist.

He said he'd fished the ocean, boy and man, for 35 years, and he knew about fog. "I know fog creates waves, because I seen it. Been out there when it happened, eh? Smooth as a mirror one second, fog rolls in, waves come up. That simple."

My experience has been different. Moored at Outer Island on Lake Superior, we woke to fog thick as pea soup shrouding the mast. We had to motor miles to return the boat on time, or pay extra. Nikki and Captain Steve plotted our course, using our starting point on the chart to Bayport--using depth, direction and speed to navigate. Meanwhile I dangled my feet over the bow, peering into the relentless gray mist, honking a foghorn-in-a-can every 15 seconds. My heart hammered, thinking that a sudden rise in the bottom of the lake, with lurking hidden rocks striking the keel, would toss me topsy-turvy overboard. The fog was thick as double-pea soup, but the lake was flat. No waves.

Another time in Acadia National Park in Maine we signed up with a ranger to take photos the next day. We woke to heavy fog, and wondered if the photo session would be held. But we dressed, grabbed our cameras, and met the ranger.

He said, "You're fortunate, because fog is the most fantastic way to take photos. You'll soon see, and get really interesting shots."

So we followed him, and began taking shots, and sure enough, his information was true. We got some really interesting shots in the fog, like this one below:

But fog is nature's gift. As Carl Sandburg wrote, it comes on little cat feet, muting the light, gentling the scene, scrubbing away reality, forming a soft surreal landscape. Fog compresses the large world into a snug hideaway, yet offers vague tantalizing glimpses of another exciting realm just beyond the edge of vision. The ethereal beauty of fog turns my thoughts to spirituality, and eternity.

In a way I guess I could agree with the old sailor. Fog can create waves--waves of trepidation, or delight.

Adventures With *Crotalus Atrox*

I've always liked snakes, even after a screaming banshee wearing my mother's dress wielded a flashing hoe, chopping a dozen sushi-sized rolls out of a garter snake that had ventured near us boys when I was five. So it was no surprise that I would share my love of serpents with Nikki and 11-year-old Steve on our inaugural trip to the North Dakota Badlands shortly after we were married.

During the trip out, I'd said I wanted to see a rattlesnake. My interest had been whetted teaching a story on the diamondback called *The Life and Death of a Western Gladiator.*

After the scenic vistas, buffalo, feral horses and prairie dogs in the Badlands, we had yet to spot any snake, much less a rattlesnake. So I'd given up, and was enjoying clambering around a butte that looked like a giant chocolate Hershey's kiss, when I jumped off a ledge onto the surrounding mud flat. And nearly landed on a three-foot rattler. With incredible speed the snake condensed itself into a beautiful ring of diamond designs as I pivoted away.

"Rattlesnake!" I yelled hoarsely. Then, "Let's catch it."

While the viper coiled, its bluish-black tongue flashed out, tasting the air. Its diabolically beautiful skull was shaped like an arrowhead. The rattle on its black-striped tail whirred and whirred like the very knell of doom, making my hair curl.

Yet I somehow said, "We have a jar in the car." Encased in glass, I could safely study it, safely, because we were not prepared for a rattlesnake interrogation, dressed in sandals, shorts, and t-shirts.

"A jar?" Nikki said. "How far is it to the nearest hospital?"

I was exasperated. I couldn't leave or the serpent would slither away. I looked around and spotted a forked stick, then pinned the beast while the thick muscular body writhed and the rattle chattered incessantly.

"Isn't it gorgeous?" I said. "Listen, this is what the rattle sounds like." Adding, "It's a sound you'll never forget."

Prairie rattlesnakes are rarely dangerous. They do not want to waste their venom on a beast like us, because we are too big. Which does not mean that they won't bite if they are provoked enough.

I flipped the snake upside down and pinned it again, while it lashed its body back and forth. "Look at its scutes. See how they work?" Scutes, inch-wide stomach plates were their means of locomotion, connected to ribs which shuttled them back and forth.

"Their fangs lay back against the roof of their mouth, and erect downwards incredibly fast as they're about to strike. That's what makes it a viper. As soon as they're born, the venom is deadly."

After studying the rattler, the smooth and colorful leathery skin, the angry eyes, I lifted the stick, and reluctantly freed it.

The rattling ceased. As it moved away, I said, "They can grow thick as a motorcycle tire."

Returning to the car, Nikki and Steve were surprisingly wary, treading carefully, searching everywhere for the rattler's family and friends.

Once in the car, all of us were exhilarated, after having observed closely such an elemental force of nature, and surviving unscathed.

A Sail Alongside Death

As a stiff breeze billowed the sails, listing our 34-foot *Easterly*, we discussed surviving the frigid water of Lake Superior that surged under our hull, hissing and gurgling this June evening. The conclusion: no longer than a few minutes.

Someone asked about storms. Our captain Steve said, "We'll listen to the radio for warnings."

The morning dawned hot, the sun relentless. Inexplicably, the radio had quit. In the calm air we ran up the front jenny sail to pick up stray puffs of air.

Steve went below. Wind moved us briskly through growing waves. The sun winked out, air cooled, and a huge dark cloud curled on the sky from behind. Talking stopped. Gusts wobbled the boat.

The captain clambered up the ladder, brushing sleep out of his eyes. "Why are we bouncing so much?"

A blast of wind teetered the boat. Cups and pots rattled. Steve glanced at the black sky and grabbed the wheel. He shouted, "Prepare to lower mainsail!"

Marble-sized raindrops perforated the water, and spattered against the boat. The storm engulfed us, whitecaps surging higher than the deck.

"The mainsail!" the captain shrieked. "Lower the mainsail or we'll go over!"

The bow rose, and plunged back into the black water. Spray sheeted high and wide. The mainsail clattered as we pulled it down, and was secured.

The bow jerked back and forth, a crazed live thing. "The jenny!" the captain screamed. "Down! Now!"

White-knuckled, I dragged myself forward, and secured a line around my waist and tied it to a cleat.

"Hurry!" Steve yelled.

A ton of black icy water engulfed me, buried me, clutched me, dragging me toward the edge of the boat. But the line held.

Spluttering, I surfaced. My hands were numb. The front sail, the jenny, crackled like gunfire, whipping the bow side to side.

I loosened the jenny's rope. The hull groaned. The sail shot out, the rope burning through my hands. While the sail snapped, I clutched the rope, my shoulder sockets rattling. I braced my feet, and pulled. It felt like a tug-of-war with death.

The wind yowled. Another foot of sail crept in. Then I saw the wave, a black monster rising. If it struck us amidships…

In a frenzy I strained against the rope. But I couldn't do it.

Then an angel touched my shoulder. Nikki's hands reached over me, and grasped the rope.

"Pull!" I screamed. The grommets rattled against the mast. A yard, two, three of wet sail plopped into my lap.

The wave blotted out the sky, and buried us. The *Easterly* groaned and shuddered like a dying animal.

I surfaced to a boat canted sideways. The mainmast nearly touched the surface, exposing the two-ton keel. For three sacred heartbeats, the boat and our lives hung in the balance.

Then the keel, white as the underbelly of a great fish, slipped into the black water. Achingly slow, the boat righted itself. Sky above, water below.

We brought in the remainder of the jenny. The waves rose and crashed, the wind threatened, but the unburdened boat followed its rudder true. The screws bit deeply, propelling us towards a small sheltered bay on Stockton Island two miles away.

And safety.

Dissolving Clouds?

A number of years ago I read a piece by a writer who claimed humans can dissolve clouds by concentrating on them. Brain waves create heat, he said, so it seems logical that heat would dissipate clouds into gas.

So on a nice sunny day I decided to try it on a few puffy clouds up in the North Dakota sky.

I spread a blanket and laid on my back, and found a small cloud about the size of a half-dollar. (Remember those coins?)

I stared at the little cloud with great concentration for a couple of minutes. Slowly it began to melt, until finally a couple of minutes later it disappeared. Holy moly! I could hardly believe it! Had I fallen asleep? Or had I actually dissolved a cloud using the heat of my brain waves?

I decided to try it again. And again it worked. For the next few days I tried again and again, and each time it worked, dissipating small clouds back into the ether.

A week later on a beach with some former students, I broached the idea to them. They'd known me for years, and they knew I came up with bizarre notions at times, so they didn't seem surprised at my claim. But a couple were doubtful.

"All right," I said. "You pick the cloud. A small one. We'll dissolve it."

They picked the cloud, a fluffy one about the size of a slice of bread, hanging above us. Five of us began to stare at the cloud.

Slowly but surely it began to mist away. After a time it disappeared. It was gone. They couldn't believe it. I still could hardly believe it. So we tried a couple more, and they met the same fate.

How was that possible? Is it the same concept as a fogged-up windshield that clears up when you blow warm air over it?

I tried dissolving parts of larger clouds, the size of several loaves of bread, hoping to punch a hole through the middle. But no dice. Nothing happened.

I tried to dissolve parts of the edges of the larger clouds, but the results were indefinite at best. Was my brainpower too puny?

Later, I read a piece where somebody said dissolving clouds wasn't possible.

I know that isn't true, because I saw it done. But--was it cause and effect? Did the clouds dissolve because I was concentrating on them? Or is it natural for small clouds to dissipate, even when nobody is looking at them? And the ones I "dissipated" would have disappeared no matter what?

Does it occur only in certain seasons and with certain kinds of clouds?

I don't know. So if anybody else out there takes this seriously and decides to try it, let me know if it works. Small clouds seem to work best.

Helicopters were never supposed to be able to fly. People were never going to land on the moon. And more. We just never know if something will work or not, until we try it.

Homeland Insecurity

One of the strangest experiences of my life--if not the strangest--occurred in Washington, D. C. a couple of years after 9-11. Also very unsettling.

After sightseeing down the long blocks and visiting the Museum of the American Indian with its fascinating old pottery, dresses, and artwork, and the National Art Gallery with paintings I'd not seen previously in real life, we emerged from the subway and were walking toward our hotel a few blocks away.

As we were passing an obviously new building that appeared to be of government vintage, judging by the large black Mercedes vehicles at the curb, with very low license plate numbers, we noticed the building was not identified. Nothing on the lawn or the building itself. Odd in a town where everything was so well-marked.

The double glass doors were locked, so we peered in. On a large thick and round rug we could make out "Homeland Security" stitched around the edge in large white letters. We made some comments, and turned away. Then I remembered the license plates, government 001 and 002, so I bent and shot pictures of them.

A moment later an official-looking agent walked around the corner holding a squawking walkie-talkie in his hand. A voice from it said, "Watch for a guy in a blue t-shirt taking pictures of our license plates."

The agent was ten feet away. I held up my camera and said, "That would be me," and walked on. We talked about the situation, which made me uneasy. Why would anybody care if their license-pates were photographed? I guess I should have asked.

At our suite at the hotel I transferred that day's photos onto Baby, our laptop computer, and talked to our friend Steve, still in bed, struggling with severe neck pain. He had not been with us.

We decided to go out for supper and promised to bring food back for Steve. When we returned I immediately noticed that my laptop was on the couch instead of the table where I had left it, and upside down. Obviously someone had been tampering with it. A small door on the bottom of the machine had been unscrewed, and not replaced properly, with one screw missing. Couldn't believe it. Who would do that, and why? Certainly not Steve, or me.

Then I remembered Homeland Security.

Steve said after we left a number of maids had come in, and had been in both of our rooms, saying they had to clean up, which seemed odd considering it was evening. One man too, he added.

I turned the computer on, and checked the photos I'd taken that afternoon. And lo! And behold! The license-plate pictures were all gone. Again, obvious. Photo numbers ending in 355 through 360 were missing.

We wondered if removing those pictures was perhaps a training exercise for a young agent who came into our suite room, doubtless with the cooperation of the hotel management, to find and remove those pictures.

But why the mess? Perhaps the thief got the word that we were returning, and had leave immediately before we came and caught him, and hadn't time to replace things properly.

Or was it a warning? *Don't mess with Homeland Security.*

What else had been stolen from our computer? Or had malware been added? Was Homeland Security now watching me?

And why such a botched job? Perhaps the door on the bottom of the computer was left open intentionally as a warning to me to not take any more "official" pictures while we were in D.C.

To this day, I don't know--and still feel uneasy when I think about it.

My Mother's Life

I can't summarize the wounds and worries and workings of 94 years of my mother's life, in a few paragraphs. But by using her own words, I hope to give you a sense of her.

Her first language was a Germans-from-the Ukraine stew of fossilized German, salted with Russian, Yiddish, maybe Ukranian. In country school, German was she was not allowed to speak German. "So during recess we'd huddle in a corner and speak German real soft, and when the teacher came near, we'd talk English real loud! As a child, to see an airplane was very strange and frightening. I used to hide until it was out of sight."

Once as a child she had a terrible stomach ache. She wrote, "My mother knew how to alleviate pain an old-fashioned way. *Brauching*. She placed a string across my body and an egg on my navel, and said a prayer. She dropped the egg into the kitchen cook stove, where it blew up with a bang--and my pain was gone!"

Her first date was with a high school classmate. "We went to the movie, and came back and sat in the kitchen, held hands, and stole a you-know-what. Can't believe I wrote this down!"

At 16 she tried to have her sister Leah teach her how to drive. "Well, my legs were short, hers long, so we couldn't agree on where to have the car seat, so I never tried after that until I was 53 years old," when she attended Bismarck Junior College, and also got her driver's license.

Her uncle August, was her favorite, despite his mental affliction. "He always spoke backwards, like *Ich die gleicha*. I you like. I never laughed at him. I just liked to hear him talk."

When asked what her college major was at Bismarck State College, she said, "College was a nine-month course, so the major thing was to get through it. Ha!" Which she did.

On a hill in the North Dakota Badlands a few years ago she saw a horse and rider coming down a hill. She yelled, "How about giving me a ride? Or else trade your young legs for my old ones."

She said she had two regrets in life: first, that she never became a nurse. But she had five boys to take care of. Second, that she didn't talk to her father when she had the chance. He lived with us for a couple of years, and he would say, "*Vass klipsch du rouse, come doh nicht und fesalla.*" What are you doing out there? Come here and talk to me." Years after he died, amid tears she said, "I didn't know what to talk about. But now I wish I would have."

A few years ago at a family reunion, she stood up and told us how proud she was of us, of the good men we'd become, of how we'd lived our lives, of how much we'd accomplished. Then she paused for a couple of beats, and ever the mother, said, "So far." It's a two-word adage by which to remember her after her February 3 death, and to live by.

Questions for Mom

My mother was a survivor. Her headstone reads, "Alma Phillibina Woehl Vossler Delzer Engelhart," as she outlived three husbands. As the years pass, more and more I remember questions I wish I would have asked her, beginning with her growing-up life.

Like everybody else in our little Germans-from-the-Ukraine community, she did not talk about the past. As I grew up there, I discovered nobody talked about the past. Ever. Not a single story. And they had many chances, as I spent hours munching ammonia cookies at the tables of newspaper customers, chatting with them while collecting for the papers. Never once did they mention anything from the past, even something so simple as, "When I was your age, in our village in the Ukraine I used to..." or anything else.

But then sixty years later during several drives of nine hours to and from Billings to visit her ailing sister, Leah, Mom told some stories. I learned how as a child she picked mostly-solid cow patties from the pastures for fuel in their farm home furnace. I heard how starting when she was 10 she made July 4 money by nabbing gophers and turning in their tails to a county office for a penny each.

She placed a noose of string around the opening of the rodents' burrows, and laid on her stomach with her head a few inches from the hole, and her arms spread on each side, holding the ends of the noose. When a gopher poked its head out of the ground, she yanked the noose tight. Goodbye gopher. Hello one cent.

She told that when her parents went to town--which happened infrequently--as soon as they were out of the yard, the 10 kids got out the sugar, cornstarch, butter, and flavoring and started making taffy. Mom, as the youngest, had the duty of watching for their parents. One time the parents returned after a half-hour for something they'd forgotten, and the kids had to hide everything away very quickly until they left again. But there was never the sense from her that they would have been penalized at all--just that that was the right thing to do.

Mom also told of how she saved her father's life. One evening she was playing upstairs and looked out the window and saw her dad working with a bull. At that second the beast got enraged at her father, and gored him and tossed him. Mom's screams brought the family running, and the older brothers got the bull away and another took her father into the hospital in Wishek, where he had surgery that saved his life.

She recalled her pet sheep that she loved very much, and used to ride around the farm. One evening after supper she wondered what they had just eaten, and to her horror discovered it had been her pet sheep, (which had never been meant to be her pet.)

She was 12 years old when the farm suffered under a plague of locusts. "They were everywhere," she said, "eating all our crops and everything green in the garden, potatoes, carrots, onions. They were all at least two inches long. Our chickens and turkeys ate so many that their stomachs grew hard, and they couldn't eat any more. But it made no difference. Plus the chicken and turkey meat was foul afterwards and could not be eaten."

So these many years later, something triggers a thought, and I look back and think, "What didn't I ask her that question?" Sometimes I wonder what other great stories from her life I certainly missed.

The Power of Stories

When I was at my wits' end with student behavior while teaching in the Writer-in-Residence program, luckily, I remembered Pat Conroy's words. Nothing I taught, nothing I did, was working, totally the opposite of all the other residencies I'd done. And in this school, most students were not a problem; except those in one fourth-grade class.

Teachers had warned me: "Incorrigible." "Can't be disciplined," "Never settle down due to their home lives: 29 of 41 came from broken homes."

But I believed I could handle them. Always had. Boy was I wrong!

They possessed little self-control and less courtesy, screeching out answers willy-nilly, clambering over each other to get to me for help, pouting and throwing tantrums.

For eight days I felt like a zoo keeper. My classroom noise had always meant kids were learning and having fun. Not here.

Then I remembered Conroy: "The most powerful words in the English language are 'Tell me a story.'"

Of course! I remembered Mom reading to me. And teachers.

But what story should I read to these incorrigibles? "Goldilocks and the Three Bears?" "Beauty and the Beast?" "Rumplestiltskin?" No. Not right.

Rather one from another residency. Paging through my folder of the best ones, I found six possibles. "*Annika*: Your name is like the smell of a first spring rain." "*A Girl In My Mind*: She's a rose, I'm the rose examiner..." "*Untitled*: I remember those quiet nights out on the porch to lay and count stars..." *Arthur*: Arthur was a very nice talking dog..." "*A Winter Night*: One winter night I heard the silence of snow as flakes fell toward the earth, and trees blew in the wind." No. None strong enough.

But the final one: *"The Killing*: To kill a beloved pet, I thought, would be a test of manhood. Blackjack, a pure black German Shepherd cross, had been mangled by the truck. I knew it had to be done but I was only 10 at the time, and Blackjack was my best friend."

Their eyes grew large. And they were quiet, and listening intently.

"The only way was to convince myself that I was a man and could help my friend. I had used a rifle many times before when my dog and I walked in the woods. Now the metal barrel felt like ice in my hands."

The fourth-graders shivered. Some bit their lower lips.

"With head hung low and tears running down my face, I loaded the gun. I stared at the vast cold loneliness of that big red barn. The door creaked when I opened it. There he was with pain in his eyes, laying in the dark corner embedded in straw.

"Memories ran through my mind, of the days we spent running through the grassy underbrush of the woods, fishing along the peaceful banks of the Sheyenne, or playing fetch with a stick.

"My dreaming of our past was hurtled back to reality by a humble whimper. It had to be done for his sake.

"After it was over, I sat down by my friend for a manly cry."

Tears streamed down the faces of every student in the room. The rest of my time with them they actively tried to learn how to write with power and passion.

From this experience I learned how powerful those English words can be: "Tell me a story."

Building a Writing Life

For the past 45 years, I have written almost every day. I make my living as a full time freelance writer, which I've wanted to do since grade seven, when I wrote my first very short book titled *The Secret of the Lost Inca Mines*. What could be greater than making up stories and getting paid for them, I thought.

It's satisfying to discover that many people like what I write, or how I write it. But that was not always so. My career began inauspiciously. In 1977 I resigned from teaching English to be a writer. Though I had never sold a single piece of writing, I was sure I knew enough and was good enough now that I could make my living at writing.

I had been learning the rudiments of the writing profession as well as writing pieces and sending them out. With zero success. During two months that summer after resigning I wrote a couple dozen pieces, sent them to *Atlantic Monthly, New Yorker, Runner's World,* and others, and waited for checks to fill my mailbox.

Unfortunately, with great dispatch editors flung my articles back to me in the SASEs (self-addressed, stamped envelopes) I was required to include if I wanted an answer. Each one included a standardized rejection slip: "Dear Writer. Thank you for sending us your work. Unfortunately it does not meet our present needs. Best of luck placing it elsewhere."

One day amidst those standardized rejection slips came a personalized one in an envelope, typed on a 3 x 5 card from the editor at *Isaac Asimov Science Fiction Magazine*.

I opened the envelope, saw the typing, and thought, "Hallelujah! Finally, an editor who sees my worth." I couldn't wait to read the card, and cash the check. So I whipped it out to finally revel in good news: "Dear Bill," it said. Personal indeed! I continued reading, and staggered as the floor fell out from beneath me. "*Dear Bill, someone has to tell you. You will never be a writer. Your prose sounds like a jackhammer outside my window at 5 AM in the morning. Get another job, and leave the writing to those who can actually write.*"

I ripped it up and tossed it into the basket, then sat down and cried. My dream of being a professional writer was dead. The editor had voiced what I feared but had never admitted--that I wasn't good enough.

So I simply quit writing, and tried to salve my grief by lots of reading, running, and playing sports. As each additional rejection trickled in, I angrily tore the envelope in half and tossed it in the wastebasket.

A month later a rejection from *Listen* magazine drifted into my box. As usual I ripped the envelope in half and turned to the wastebasket only to notice edges of green paper inside the envelope. My mouth dropped open as I pulled out a now-two-piece check for $50 ($200 today) for an article ironically titled, *Are You Your Own Worst Enemy?* The envelope also contained a letter saying, "Please send more." Sky-high, I cried again. I hadn't been wrong!

The proof is in selling almost everything I've written for the past 40 years. I've written features, interviews, anecdotes, poetry, short stories, even a play, for magazines as *Toy Farmer, Reader's Digest, Houseboat, Arizona Highways, Saturday Evening Post, Sr. Perspective,* and 230 others.

But my most potent joy has emanated from writing essays. They require me to think, often deeply, to dig the ore of words from the rock, and tumble them in order onto the paper to make the piece work. Or sometimes dig out diamonds of exactly the right words that add beauty, and make the sentences sing.

That 3 x 5 card experience taught me powerful lessons: pay more attention to my inner drive than words from outside, work hard, learn the craft, and never ever give up on a dream, no matter how difficult, even impossible, it might seem.

The Effects of Beautiful Writing

Beautiful writing has always moved me, like this line from Ray Bradbury's short story "The Dragon:" *Now only the night moved in the souls of the two men bent by their lonely fire in the wilderness; darkness pumped quietly in their veins and ticked silently in their temples and wrists.*

Reading those words, suddenly I am no longer in my comfortable living-room chair, but transported outdoors to squat on a rough log next to a crackling fire in the cool darkness, feeling anxious, wondering where the next gallery of words will lead me.

Then there is Annie Dillard in her book "An American Childhood": *Time itself bent you and cracked you on its wheels.*

Or Thomas Wolfe in his book "Of Time and the River": *Where the river, the dark and secret river, full of strange time, is forever flowing by us to the sea.*

For years I read those golden nuggets of sentences, hoping their proficiency would rub off on me, and I would mine veins of words to write like them. After much practice, I did create some: My memoir, "Days of Wonder" has: *The first time my father died, I was but a mote of starlight hurtling earthward from a far-flung galaxy.*

Then my piece in "The Boundary Waters Journal:" *One brittle-bone night on the Gunflint, my wife and I stamped and shivered on a trail beneath the dark hood of the sky, watching, through the billowing clouds of our breath as the pink aurora borealis fingered the horizon.*

After I wrote each sentence, I felt elated. Yes! I could do it! I could write beautifully! And I was hopeful that by producing more lovely sentences--essentially practicing--they would become easier to create regularly. But I didn't find that that method worked for me.

Those writers--Bradbury, Dillard, Wolfe, Ackerman--possess, I think, a larger part of the writing brain than I possess but feebly. Call it the figurative language section, into which they can seem to tap easily and frequently, and each time stunning writing gushes out. Not so with me. First I struggle to find my minuscule figurative language area in my brain, and when I tap into it, a mere weak trickle of somewhat-striking words dribbles out.

Creating gorgeous writing takes great effort and lots of time. It requires repetition, rethinking and rewriting numerous times--attempting to snap the correct puzzle pieces of words into jigsaws of sentences--without the corresponding picture on the box--to complete the thought exactly right, and strikingly. Then days later a reread most likely discovers that at least one broken word cannot be fixed, or snapped back into place.

Thus more time and effort, until finally all the words click nicely, not as powerful as those of Bradbury et. al, but good enough.

Most beautiful writing requires comparisons I especially like to work, called metaphors, as in the italicized sentence above, or similes, comparisons using 'like' or 'as,' as below: In her book, "Harpist in the Wind," Patricia A. Mikillip writes, *His body lay like a fragment of rock on the floor of the mountain.*

Or Thomas Wolfe in "Look Homeward Angel:" *Their wild laughter leaped like freed hounds.*

Over the years I have come up with similes that I like: *His smile lay like a warm arm across my shoulder.* Or *The wind whined like a live beast on the spoor of prey as it moaned along the narrow siding, snuffling for weaknesses to insert its frigid -40 degree snout.*

Why use figurative language at all? To craft unforgettable vivid imagery with intricate and subtle rhythms of striking writing that enriches our imaginations, and creates ways to appeal directly to our senses. Figurative language can help us see the world differently, which might aid us in comprehending difficult writing, and lead us to continue a piece we might have abandoned, written less well, like Diane Ackerman in "The Enchanted Loom:" *If we needed to remember how to work the bellows of the lungs or the writhing python of digestion, we'd be swamped...and there'd be no time left for buying cute socks.*

As Pat Conroy summarized in "The Writer's Digest," *Good writing is the hardest form of thinking. It involves the agony of turning profoundly difficult thoughts into lucid form, then forcing them into the tight-fitting uniform of language, making them visible and clear.*

A Little Froggy Excitement

I've witnessed memorable moments in nature: sandhill cranes walking calmly 10 feet in front of our car; a snapping turtle on the road hissing; an eagle soaring over our heads while we're on our bicycles, and snagging a dead squirrel 50 feet ahead; chunks of dead willow exploding outward, obscuring the blurring red-topped head of the pileated woodpecker seeking its lunch.

Nature is filled with opportunities to witness incidents like these, natural occurrences to make us smile, to fill us with joy and awe, granting us respite from our worries, creating memories we will never forget. Best of all, they're free.

Luckily, you don't always need to know *where* to look--you only need *to be looking*. Like the other night when moths patted our picture window with their wings, breaking my reading reverie. I cocked my head, hearing the pock of other sweaty insects trying to batter into our air-conditioned comfort.

And then--I heard the soft plunkety-plunk of tiny feet against the window--a tree frog. Stuck to the outside glass, its arms raised as though signaling a touchdown, he gazed inside, his throat working as though muttering, "Whoa! Lookit all those books! And a stupid cat. Nyah nyah! Just try to catch me, fur face."

Which Anjo did, leaping onto a chair, pawing at the glass between her and the frog, tasting the window for good measure, before sitting and staring at the frog in puzzlement.

People know about poison dart tree frogs whose deadly venom, similar to curare, is used for blowgun darts, and also to save many human lives as an anesthetic in open-heart surgery.

Less is known about our shy 2 ½-inch tree frog. His only poison is his tongue, so to speak (like some people) revealed when a moth, high on seeing the light, danced within striking distance. The tongue snapped out three inches, nailing the moth. Quicker than the insect could scream "Oops!" it was dragged into the frog's mouth, the tip of a wing wriggling belatedly for a second before disappearing altogether.

The tree frog's three-inch tongue is a popgun in the frog world compared to the possible 12-inch howitzer of an adult frog. But it does the job, thank you.

Having gobbled that big moth, I figured the frog must be sated, because a pair of teenage moths, daring each other, kept sallying back and forth within what I considered range of the frog's tongue, yet escaping without getting caught.

Evidently tree frogs can only fire their tongues forward. The frog adjusted himself, patting the glass like a rock climber feeling for the next handhold, edging into position by increments, pat, pat, pat (I imagined the glass squeaking under his webbed feet) until he created a straight-ahead shot. Flick. Another over-exuberant moth seeking enlightenment was unexpectedly called home.

Another memorable incident to add to my Rolodex of nature's experiences.

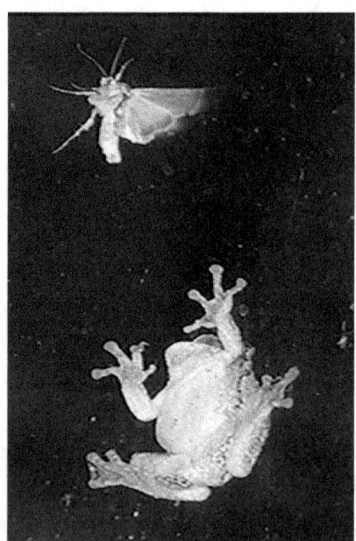

Tree frog and an insect lunch.

The Ecstasy of Nature

One night as I lay on a blanket in the grass, searching the black sky for the sudden jewelry of falling stars, I was reminded of many gifts I have been endowed with, mostly the ecstasy of nature.

This night was another one, the sky above pockmarked with bright white holes of stars poking through the firmament, as though an gigantic unseen fire burned in a chasm beyond the blackness.

I have always loved nature, ever since as a 7-year-old kid living across the street from a great four-square-block of land, a seemingly-empty lot, which teemed with every form of nature: butterflies, fireflies; frogs, toads; *marrivarich* (stinkweed), pigweed; gophers, mice; sparrows, robins; ravine, plain; water, sand, all of which I could examine at my leisure, and learn from them.

As I lay in the grass gazing at the gifts of abounding stars, I suddenly felt I was levitating upward into the sky, rising toward the stars and getting so close I felt I could grab them with my bare hands and drop them one by one into my shirt pocket, brightening up the night around me. An incredible, impossible feeling.

Just then a meteor smacked the atmosphere far above, a fast white surgical knife-slice in the darkness, filling my heart with joy.

That something so small, the size of a pea or smaller, like most meteors, could create a bright one-second stripe seen for up to 600 miles (if it struck near the horizon), was amazing.

After a while a male great horned owl on the right voiced a low booming hoot-hoot-hoot, followed seconds later by the female's higher hoots to the left--perhaps saying, "Couple of mice over here," one might have said, and answering "Big fat rabbit here."

Shortly a coyote took up howling, its voice rising so high I thought it would crack, then joined by an additional trio of coyotes, a wonderful yet painful lamenting quartet. I shivered.

When a pair of meteors scratched the sky, I wondered how old those meteors were. Perhaps old as time itself? And from where did they arise? Probably the asteroid belt, where most of them come from, a collection of rocky and metal objects that orbit the sun between Mars and Jupiter. Were they former pieces of other planets--or even stars?

I felt small with the immensity of it all. Yet filled with astonishment. Moments later a sliver of moon peeked out from where it had been clothed in silver fog. My glass of wonder kept overflowing. The world around me felt like a great dark cathedral, and to honor it I felt like I had to speak in whispers. Everything big and small around me began to take on new and deeper meanings.

I conjectured about the ancient peoples who spent many nights outside, and saw the same stars, gazing upward, curious what they were. Then the cries of surprise or fear when meteors streaked across the sky. What could they mean? Perhaps they thought it was magic. Some believed they were eternal lights representing the souls of their lost ones in the afterlife, or that they were heavenly signs.

Symbolizing that, in *King Lear*, Shakespeare has Gloucester say, "These late eclipses in the sun and moon portend no good to us." And in *Julius Caesar*, on the fateful morning of her husband's murder, Calpurnia says, "When beggars die, there are no comets seen; The heavens themselves blaze forth the death of princes."

Oddly enough, in real life in July 44 BC after Caesar's assassination on the Ides of March, a great comet appeared in the sky, perhaps the brightest daytime comet ever. Caesar's Comet they called it, or the Great Comet of 44 BC. It coincided with games held to honor Caesar. Romans felt it meant Caesar had become a god and ascended to heaven."

From time immemorial, the nighttime skies have meant huge things to different ancient people. And to modern people, like me, lying on a blanket in the grass.

Heavenly Orb

Homewrecker! I had never been accused of that dishonor before, but no other term seemed accurate for someone who tore down the living quarters of an innocent fellow-traveler of the planet--*Argiope*, a yellow and black orb spider. With a body shaped like a miniature football, about the size of a quarter, *Argiope* sprawled complacently in the middle of a beautiful shiny web the size of a dinner plate in the bush by our front steps. Her legs were very long, "giving (her) a most menacing look," Wikipedia says.

Overnight she built her web. I hope she received time-and-a-half as it was gorgeous, dewdrops on its lines glittering like a lit chandelier in the early morning sunlight.

She had attached several lines side by side to our soffit, floated down three feet to affix the other ends to the shaft of a leaf, probably whooping in a high-pitched, reedy voice, "Wheeeee!" as she dropped. She crawled up and dove down a dozen more times to thicken this main support.

Below the center of the web, where she took up residence, she weaved a thick zigzaggy white silk pattern resembling a zipper, and as wide, down to the edge of the web. This *stabilimentum* identifies the five species of orb-weaver, only one of which occupies Minnesota, and is built by larger orb spiders. Nobody knows the zipper's use. Hypotheses include web stabilization, visibility so birds won't wreck it, light reflection to attract insects, or camouflage for the spider. Perhaps a little bit of each?

Instinctively, she attached perhaps 30 more points to firmly anchor the round web. How many? I don't know for sure, because before counting I quickly brought down the house.

I hadn't meant to. I wanted a close-up photo of the spider hammocking in the center of the web before she skittered away. But when leaves obscured my view, I pulled the branch out of the way. *Pling plang plung,* the guy wires snapped, and the web collapsed into an unruly pile of strings.

With a multiple glance at me with her eight eyes, filled with annoyance, she turned into the bush, never to appear again.

Information about *Argiope* from *Wikipedia* explained why: *(Argiope's) proficiency at nighttime hunting and propensity to enjoy insects makes them the ultimate in the way of mosquito zappers. Keep (Argiope) around, and you'll notice the mosquito population dwindle in the dusk-to-nighttime hours.*

Perhaps it was only my fancy, but the number of mosquitoes seemed to tick up shortly after *Argiope* disappeared.

The Life and Death of Chrissie Chrysops

She was born on a late spring morning, hatched from an egg in a mass glued to the moist underside of a milkweed leaf. Hundreds of brothers and sisters were born with her.

They plopped into the half-inch-deep puddle scooped in the marshy mud below the leaf. Each Chrysops larva was half an inch long, and slimmer than a pencil lead.

Nobody cared whether Chrissie lived or died. Her tiny brain was very dull. She had no arms or legs. She propelled herself about her small murky world with pseudopods, or false feet. Her skin was leathery. Nearly everything that flew in the air or swam in the water was her enemy, including her siblings, who would without remorse devour her for their next meal.

But she didn't know that. She knew nothing at all. She was aware of her own existence, the total sum of her knowledge.

In the dim soft jungle of water and mud, Chrissie fought daily to win the hunger lottery. The prize was survival. Her prey included worms, snails, and insect larvae, especially the crane fly.

One by one her siblings succumbed, until she alone of the clutch remained. Although she was far more agile than she looked, she was not strong, or fast, or intelligent, yet her tiny spark of life stayed alight through luck. She grew fat.

Each day she felt stronger. Then one day an odd lassitude gripped her. Shortly she suffered an irresistible urge to burrow deep into the cool mud. Once covered by the wet darkness, a waking coma overtook her. Strange forces worked inside her body.

When she awoke, chilled, she wriggled to the surface.

She was different, but she couldn't have said how. With her new hairy legs she crawled up the milkweed stem, and stood triumphantly, her antennae waving, atop the very leaf under which she had been born.

She had been recreated. Her senses hummed. She lifted her clear wings to the sun, noting their movement with the 20,000 facets in her large iridescent green, yellow, and gold-banded eyes. In the soothing warm rays, her new body slowly hardened.

After a time, her thorax pulsed with rushes of power, until her wings beat the air 90 times a second, lifting her off the leaf. She felt a flash of rapture. The milkweed below receded. Her metamorphosis was complete.

She reveled in the pure joy of her new powers, racing and dipping, adjusting to the nudges of air currents, dive-bombing the milkweed, testing her brown and yellow body.

She was a lovely and fearful quarter-inch-long miniature flying machine. She smelled a heavy sweet odor in the air. Her gastric juices bubbled. In a pasture she spotted six beasts, swishing their hairy tails back and forth. Her first hunt!

She chose a big strong roan, and buzzed in for a landing on its rump. Its swishing tail snapped down, sweeping her away.

After two more near-disasters, she settled further forward on the horse, wary of the seeking tail, but its sound was now sweet victory as it swished and missed her.

She unsheathed a pair of mandibles, broad, toothed daggers. She plunged her piercing stylets through the hide. The horse leaped, whinnying, smacking its tail uselessly time and again. Chrissie sawed up and down with her mandibles. She was anchored, her sucking tubes in the damaged tissues while her powerful head pump drew up the blood, thinned by her own saliva to prevent coagulation.

She did not know this, of course. She simply did it. A few moments later she unrolled her tongue to lap up the blood.

The horse stamped and groaned, shivering, but Chrissie hung on until she was satiated. Then without a backward glance, she buzzed up into the warm rays of the sun.

She had much to learn. Deerflies cannot fly without the sun's heat on cool mornings or evenings, but the heat was a double-edged sword. Within seconds, she overheated. If she had not swooped down under a cool leaf, she would have died of sunstroke.

At maturity she was three-quarters of an inch long, and diabolically beautiful. She roamed her airy kingdom with the haughtiness of a queen. Her iridescent eyes aided her in finding, in full color, food, enemy birds, rivals.

One day in early fall, she spotted a male deer fly with fetching green-gold eyes that met in the middle, like those of all males, making him look as though he wore goggles. She was drawn to him like an iron filing to a magnet. In the cool shade they dipped and soared, dancing to the innate, age-old rhythms.

Alone, she laid her clutch of eggs in a puddle of water shadowed by milkweed plants. Afterwards, giddily, she arced and twisted in the air, full of joy, until she grew hot and tired and hungry.

She spotted a two legged creature, swooped down, landed among the sparse hairs on the leg, and bit.

A hand flashed down with great speed, but to her, it was slow motion. She lifted off backwards, noting the welling of crimson blood, hearing the screech.

Suddenly the hand swatted the air, not where she had been, or where she was, but where she would be going. A worthy opponent! And a game to test her mettle!

She circled about the creature's head. A second hand appeared. Chrissie almost got hit, so intent was she on the first, and so filled with the joy of competition.

She discovered the hands could alter speed, faster or slower, unlike the clumsy tails of horses. The hands also worked in conjunction. She darted away to elude their concerted attack. A stray gust of air knocked her off course. She struck against a building.

She tumbled, dazed, and felt herself dangling in the air, sticky filaments crisscrossing her wings, back, legs. She would make short work of them!

She revved her powerful wings. She leaped off the wall. Freedom! For but a split second.

The thin strings jerked her back. She was not free. A strong taste rose in her throat. Her wings had always rescued her!

She rested, her abdomen pulsing. The wind strummed the web in a rhythmic, calming way. She saw the garden spider, and met its glaring red eyes. It crept toward her. Half her size, yet its malevolent, confident posture started a trickle of fear deep inside her.

Chrissie felt more movement. To her left, another larger spider advanced, the female, twice the size of its mate with multiple red eyes and an evil black body.

Desperately, Chrissie churned her wings. She batted against the siding, and bounced deeper into the web. The filaments were thin, but strong as tensile steel. She had to get loose!

She vibrated her wings faster and faster until they were a blur. She gnashed her mandibles, thrusting them out to intimidate the spiders. They retreated, crouching just out of reach in a haughty manner, as though they'd witnessed this before. Chrissie hung upside down, tired and breathless.

Suddenly one the spiders glided along the filaments, closing in on her. Chrissie felt a sudden stinging in the tip of her left front leg. She yanked it away. Another sting in her right leg.

Numbness began to sweep over her. Her wings barely moved. A deep silence wrapped itself around her. The spiders glared at her, their front legs twitching like witch's fingers.

They crept closer, darting in for another sting. And another. For a moment she fell asleep.

A sudden jolt of the web awakened her. Something settled on her abdomen. Another sharp prick.

Something probed deep inside her. She could not pull away. She felt their tools moving red hot inside her, the greasy heat of their salivas turning her innards liquid. She tried to thrash. But she was paralyzed.

She felt her abdomen wilt as the spiders slowly sucked the life juice out of her. No more soaring, no more diving, no more delicious blood.

She fell into a troubled sleep, surrounded by an ever-creeping darkness.

An Evening Visitor

On any given day our back yard is a zoo of free-running and unruly denizens. They sneak in night and day to cram their maws with sunflower seeds and suet, and occasionally each other, as beasts of every stripe show up--birds, cats, dogs, mice, chipmunks, gophers, squirrels, raccoons, wild turkeys (a flock of 17), rabbits, deer, and an opossum.

Wild animals like the opossum often appear in our bird feeder area. I watch them through my office window all day.

One evening, getting to know two teenage Japanese girls, we were trading stories and life experiences. At one point the girls spoke with reverence of the sacred foxes in their culture.

In Japan foxes, called *kitsune,* are believed to be intelligent, possessing magical abilities that increase with age, and are also believed to assume human form. Like folklore of many cultures, some Japanese folktales indicate *kitsune* trick people. But other Japanese stories portray them as faithful guardians, friends, lovers, and wives.

I told the girls I grew up on the prairie, spotting foxes from time to time, shy and beautiful and graceful animals, adding, "Yet during our years in this house, with all the wild animals out here, you'd think we would have seen a fox. But we never have."

A few minutes later I rose to refill lemonades. On the way to the kitchen I glanced out the picture window, and froze in disbelief. Twenty feet away, across the patio on the verge of the lawn, stood a red fox, his wide sharp ears raised. He tossed his head and looked at me, as though to say, "Tell the girls. They're far from home. It will be a nice surprise for them."

Partially paralyzed with surprise. I managed to motion to our guests, whispering that a fox now graced our front yard. They frowned at each other for a few seconds, then at the sight of their sacred animal their jaws dropped and their eyes widened. For a few breathless moments the fox faced us, then turning full length, as if to display its red shoulders, sleek form, and triangle of black at the tip of the tail, it bounded away.

We all let out our breaths. Our animated conversation speculated on the chance of encountering a fox for the first time on the night we were entertaining two girls to whom the animal was sacred. "It's like he knew you were here," I said.

The next morning as we parted, the girls thanked us for housing them, "and for the gift of *kitsune,*" one said, her eyes shining.

A largesse to us all.

The Big Opossum Stops By

One night through my office window I caught movement in our lilac tree, which is festooned with bird-feeders and suet--a chubby opossum chowing down mealworm suet, which I'd bought to attract pileated woodpeckers.

The first opossum I'd ever seen had been sprawled on the road 15 years ago. Opossums in Stearns County? I thought the loathsome beasts were strictly southerners.

But it was an opossum, with that long tail like a dead worm, and a ratlike snout. I figured it was an aberration, having mistakenly hitchhiked with a returning snowbird.

In New Zealand, our party kept passing numerous unidentified lumps of road kill on the highway. Rabbits? Wallabies?

After examining one, I noted the snout looked vaguely opossumish. But it sported a thick rich coat of brownish-black fur and a long furry tail. Moments later locals confirmed they were opossum, wildly furry, unlike the Virginia opossum of the United States.

Back home, suet was disappearing at an alarming rate, so I rapped the window. The opossum ignored me, chomping happily away. I raced outside and snapped a hasty picture while the opossum climbed down and ambled off into the darkness. Unconcerned. Not even a glance at me. As if I didn't exist.

That irked me, the ambling. Squirrels, rabbits, chipmunks all jumped when I pounded on the window, squeaking "How high?"

Not the Big O. Adding insult to injury, the next morning the entire suet block was gone. I could practically hear him chortling.

Aargh. Lunching is fine. I'll share. But outright thievery, no.

This meant war. I hung up another mealworm suet, this time in a closed wire tray. Take that, vile beast!

The next day, it did--take the suet. The wire tray lay open and empty. Big O two, me zero.

Opossums are North America's only marsupials, pouched mammals, like kangaroos. They rarely contract rabies, and are practically impervious to bites of poisonous snakes.

And are surprisingly beneficial, often scouring the neighborhood of vermin, like a U.S. Marshal ridding the environs of outlaws, before moving on.

At Big O's next appearance I ran outside and he scurried to the top branches of our lilac tree. He'd bested me before, but now I had the upper hand. With great ardor I shook his branch until he hung only by his paws, then plopped into the snow, and scurried behind lawn chair folded against the side of the house.

Despite ingesting tons of free suet, he looked small and vulnerable. I began to feel sympathy for him, being harassed by the big bad ogre. He had good points. He just wanted food like the birds. So why harass him?

When I saw him trembling, my heart went out to him, and my hand automatically reached down and petted him. (Possums never attempt to bite or defend themselves, instead playing dead.) He allowed me two slow strokes, then ambled off, never to be seen again.

But he left his mark. Unlike New Zealand opossums, whose fur combined with merino wool woven into coats that sell for hundreds of dollars, this little fellow had a different value. He made me think about my biases.

The Bonus of the Pileated

The first bonus of the pileated woodpecker was offered to me one morning as I was seeking alone time from visitors. I slipped out and parked my van next to a slough to write, and see wildlife.

Opening the windows, I inhaled cool fecund air and was about to take up my pen when shadows flashed over the van. Two big black birds with flaming red caps coasted into sight over the slough, their underwings very white.

I'd never seen them before. For big birds they landed gracefully on the gray trunk of a dead ash tree 20 feet away.

They lurched up the tree, attacking the trunk with admirable fervor. Chips, nay veritable chunks, of wood sprayed into the air and rained down into the water. Aha! Woodpeckers.

My breath caught. I froze, lest I spook them. They were one of nature's free wonders, a surprise and beautiful stunning creatures, like remnants from primal forests of the Triassic.

Mesmerized, I watched as they whacked away at the wood with their sharp chisel-like beaks. (I found out later they have special yellow feathers covering their nostrils, preventing inhalation of wood dust.) With their long sticky tongues they ingested carpenter ants and beetle larvae, their favorites (they will eat fruits and nuts).

Later I discovered they were pileated woodpeckers (pile- or pill-eeated, *Driocopus pileatus*, 16-19 inches tall, with a wingspan of 26-30 inches), the largest woodpecker in North America since the demise of the ivory-billed, except for Mexico's imperial woodpecker.

Seeing the pileateds lightened my heart, and I wanted to see them more often. But how? Erect quarters by a slough? Purchase hordes of carpenter ants or beetle larvae?

Pileated woodpeckers--aka Woody Woodpeckers--visit my bird feeders almost every day. At one time I had eight of them.

By coincidence, I had started supplementing black-oil sunflower seeds on my feeder with suet. A week later I heard a wild high-pitched but slow *kuk, kuk, kuk* cry, followed by rapidly-escalating *kuk-kuk-kuk-kuks* that transported me to primeval jungles. A male pileated swooped in, a slash of red across its cheek. My jaw dropped.

He paused on the branch to consider the five options on today's suet menu: hot pepper, pecan, raisin, mealworm, and peanut butter delight. He fixed me with his wild-eyed stare, his head feathers rumpled by the breeze, sampled mealworm and pecan as hors d'oeuvres, moving to the entree, peanut butter delight, which he worked over for five minutes.

Over the next few years, pileateds became staples at my bird feeder, often visiting the suet cafe several times a day. Each time I simply had to stop and partake of their beauty and majesty. I learned to recognize at least ten adults and two young, and every time I saw them--the red cap of the male covering the top of the head almost to the bill, the female's grayish to brown forehead--my heart was gladdened.

That all changed this summer. They stopped coming. Weeks went by. Months. I doubled their favorite suets, to no avail. I was crushed. Occasionally on a walk I heard the cry or drumming, or spotted its distinctive undulating woodpecker flight. But my cupboard remained bare of pileateds. Had they found better food?

At times I gazed sadly out my window, wondering what had happened to them. In late November, my heart caught in my throat when out of the blue I heard the *kuk-kuk-kuk* once more. A young pileated dropped in and wrestled with the suet, eating his fill. On Thanksgiving day two more showed.

Now they've returned in full force. Every day I can look forward to another of these free gifts from nature, the pileated woodpeckers, all topped in a Christmasy red bow.

Notes From the Animals

A squirrel left a note for me in the new-fallen snow the other day. While my breath ballooned, I knelt to examine the writing.

"This way," the note said in its dainty tracery in the white snow blanket, "Come along. Observe my early-morning rounds."

Not wanting to disappoint my visitor, and figuring something was up, I followed the note--delicate tracks pressed into the snow, with occasional brushings of the tail where the squirrel stopped for a better view.

I stood for better perpsective. The tracks were clear, etched in the snow, dashing pit-a-pat hither and yon, from tree to acorn cache. I followed them until they were crossed by another delicately-written note, which I decided to read, getting sidetracked. Now I see the snow, white as a new sheet of paper, has many notes written across its pristine surface.

Ah yes, a mouse? Tiny tracks. One second there was nothing, the next second a tracery of fine lace was etched across the sward, as though it had apparated, perhaps from Hogwart's. The steps tippy-toed across the concrete to the bottom of a garage door, then a little ruffle appeared in the snow where the mouse had put his nose down for a smell of the sunflower seeds inside, then hied off to the next door to see if there might be a weakness there. After that, the mouse filigreed its tracks around the corner of the garage towards the raspberry patch.

I found a rabbit's track, distinctive with its elongated back hopping legs, creating a track so long the feet appeared to be dragging, like a schoolboy heading reluctantly to school, perhaps.

For a dozen steps I followed the track, reading each note, until I paused and frowned. Now this was odd. By the four sets of rear-foot tracks, all stamped in from the same spot, with each set turned in a different direction, like cogs in a broken gear, the rabbit stopped quite suddenly, and surveyed its kingdom. I knelt and examined them more closely, trying to read the meaning.

Of course. Now I can read the note clearly. Front paws touched down only in two spots, which means the rabbit stood for a while on its hind legs, shifting, paws held in front, sensing danger. I can imagine its fur white as it stood, its nose twitching, its eyes darting as its ears funneling in the sounds of the wind and the granules of pattering snow. Hoping against hope.

Running into the crafty and cunning fox is not a good omen for the rabbit. Doubtless the rabbit saw the fox. Certainly smelled it. The rabbit received its own message on the wind. Fox! Up and away!

The rest of the message is written more clearly. Another dozen steps for me and I see the pad tracks of a fox. A red fox, by its prints. Because of abundant foot-hairs, the red fox's prints show little fine detail, just parts of the toes and heel pads, with the diagnostic slightly-curved bar across the fore heel pad.

Now the handwriting--or footwriting--is more crabbed and furious, the tracks no longer slow and steady. The words are smudged by haste.

Here the rabbit's hind legs skidded in its urgency to escape its predator. Here the larger fox tracks overlap the tracks of the rabbit. The writing comes fast and furious then, the spaces between the rabbit tracks further between as he skedaddled.

But the fox's foot pads lengthened too. I gazed up ahead, and decided not to follow those tracks; I'm afraid I know the plot too well, and the ending of that story.

I rose and gazed into the blue wash of the sky. Often I've wished birds would have wing prints. You can see their prints on the ground, skinny and wicked-looking like the hand of a three-fingered witch, but I wished for tracks across the sky, magnificent loops and dives and swerves, perhaps in different colors for different birds, scraped across the sky, like jet contrails.

But until then, on the powdered ground surrounding me, there is enough reading material, enough notes from our animal friends, to keep me busy for a long time.

A Mug Only a Mother Could Love

   Which turkey should we choose? I wondered. Not from the frozen section of a grocery store, but cresting a hill north of Rockville. Perhaps one of the eight turkeys trotting across the road ahead of us? Or one of the other 25 in the flock in the ditches?

   They climbed steadily up the brown ditch onto the road looking like a very large dotted line, heads bobbing with each step. A turkey fashion runway. I imagined an announcer: "Sauntering down the roadway now, dressed stylishly in dark feathery garb..."

   One day out my office window I glanced up into the big black eye of a tom turkey peering in. His ugly head looked like it was stitched together by a mad scientist. Beak yellow tipped, then light red, then black. The snood, a fleshy whitish-red protuberance atop the beak looked unnervingly like a distant hairy volcano. The skull flesh was angry red, as though the turkey had been plucking out scattered wild black hairs in white or blue spots. A wrinkled red wattle dangled beneath the neck. A mug only a mother could love.

A mug only a mother could love.

Slowly I raised my camera and snapped a couple of photos before he bent down out of sight.

In 1784, when Benjamin Franklin proposed that a turkey would have been a better choice as the national bird instead of a bald eagle, could he have ever seen a wild turkey up close?

I stood and gazed out the window. I was astonished to see a flock of 17 wild turkeys beneath my bird feeders, pecking up sunflower seeds. They seemed comfortable with my watching them for long minutes.

They started to grow on me. Not counting the turkey head, I decided, these birds really were majestic, even beautiful, with curved rows of feathers on their sides like ridges of dark sand tossed up on a beach. Each bird was distinctive, in body feather design, or whitish or reddish spots, or occasional iridescent areas. The wingtips alternated rows of brown and white.

That winter I often saw the turkeys lurking outside my window, digging in the snow, pecking sunflower seeds. But as time passed, their numbers dwindled--15, 13, nine, only one. Then none.

I pondered why. Cars? No bodies or feathers on the street where they crossed to my feeders. Weather? Not that harsh. Mobility, moving like modern Americans? I finally put it down to a successful hunter--maybe fox. Nature red in tooth and claw.

But I missed them, their slow stately walk, their large bodies on spindly legs, their aura of confidence.

These memories flitted in my mind as I pulled to the side of the road, trying to decide my next move with these strutting meals.

If I stomped on the accelerator, I'd probably thump half a dozen into fowline heaven, and we only needed one. We'd have to scald them, pick off the pin feathers, and gut them.

Plus, the possibility of damage to my car grill--or windshield was real. Out-of-pocket expenses. And maybe there is some arcane law against running down helpless turkeys with a car. Not sporting.

Nah. As Emily Litella used to say, "Never mind."

So we sat in the car and counted them as blessings as we watched them cross the road--all 28 of them--magnificent specimens of Mother Nature, reminding us to be thankful this season for family, friends, life, readers--and wild turkeys.

A Rare Bird

In a pasture years ago, a friend and I spotted an albino gopher. Being white was marvel enough, but for a bonus it raced in a circle--backwards, and zipped down its hole, tail first. Quite the opposite of flickertails, which flicked their tail at us disdainfully before disappearing into their holes.

Besides the oddity of running backwards, the experience alerted me to albinos. The next albino I saw was an albino bison, sacred to many Indian tribes. It stood atop an embankment along I-94 near Jamestown, North Dakota, home of the world's largest buffalo. I climbed the embankment and shot photos of the white beast through the fence, which was reveling in the breeze that helped it fight off hordes of black flies.

Albinos of any kind are rare, which perhaps explains my next overzealous foray into albino-ness. At a Cold Spring stoplight I spotted a wild albino duck swimming in a small pond next to the road. It turned away as I caught a glimpse of its pink eye--the sure sign of albino-hood. I was excited.

Crouching, I crept through the grass so I wouldn't startle it into flight before I could get photos. The glare off the water prevented me from seeing the pink eyes.

As camouflage, I used a row of thick bushes along the verge of the pond to sneak closer and get clearer shots. I snapped a few pictures, then moving slowly, careful not to disturb it, I videoed it while it continued to swim in a small circle, ignoring me.

Back home I loaded the media into the computer and called Nikki. "Look what I shot!" I said. "An albino duck! You don't see many of them around! In fact, I've never seen another one."

As I clicked through the photos, something about the duck seemed odd. But I couldn't place what. Except that the eyes no longer seemed pink; well, they definitely weren't pink, which probably slightly altered my earlier classification of the duck. But something else bothered me too.

I enlarged the photo, and was amazed at the sharp outline of the feathers, but with my new camera, I expected great detail.

In the video, we watched the duck swim its little arc. Back and forth. But no paddling feet. Strange. Yet it continued swimming.

Well, not really swimming. More like--drifting. In a pattern. The same pattern. With the same movement. Time after time. As though it was--tethered.

We both reached the same conclusion at the same time.

"That's not an albino duck. It's not even a duck! It's a--a--a--white decoy!"

For at least another year the decoy was still there, a constant reminder of my folly. Doubtless a lesson was be learned from this incident--perhaps "look before you leap."

But I choose to view it as an opportunity to test my emotional components to see if they are still working right: curiosity, surprise, excitement, wonder, satisfaction, more excitement, bafflement, discovery, surprise again, and chagrin.

Yup, they all still work.

This "world's largest buffalo" at Jamestown, North Dakota is 26 feet high, 46 feet long, and weighs 40 tons.

Sudden Silence

    I learned a little lesson in our back yard a couple of springs ago. Actually two lessons. One learned, and one renewed.

    Following a spring storm, an unusual bird appeared at my feeders. One I'd never seen before. It attacked the peanut butter suet with abandon, as though it had not eaten in days. I studied it for a while, and realized it was one that I had never seen before. "'Wow!" I thought, "that's not a downy," though of similar size and relatively similar markings. I snapped a couple of photos, and with those snapshots, a quick check of the bird book indicated it was a rare red-naped sapsucker. Wow! How exciting!

    I am a sucker for new birds, ever since teaching "*The Scarlet Ibis*" by James Hurst, a short story about a bird and a boy who were driven off course, and died.

    My new bird perfectly fit the bill of that mental narrative. The poor thing had been pushed into new territory far from its normal home in the Rocky Mountains, 900 miles away. I was excited about identifying this rare guest. I was grateful and even more excited when a male, with a double dose of brilliant red on a skullcap and under its chin, and a white streak on the edge of its folded wing, returned to my feeders regularly. And then the female.

    What a thrill to be in the thrall of a beautiful distinctive bird like *Sphyrapicus nuchalis*. During this time in the back yard I kept hearing a continual chorus of songs, like a fast distant squeaky wheel, alternating high and low, *YEEP yeep YIPE yeep yeep YEEP yipe yipe*, over and over.

    I tracked it to a hole in our dead poplar where I found four nestlings. They looked as if they'd gone through a dozen rounds in the boxing ring, punching each other with their stubby little wings, causing bulging black eyes and various body discolorations.

When they heard me, they leaped into paroxysms of joy. They jabbed their beaks into the air, their maws wide, tongues wiggling, figuring I was Ma with vittles. After waggling a finger near their beaks, I figured it wasn't fair to fool them, so I retreated.

The next day I returned with my camera, hearing "feed me!"--until I was five feet away. Suddenly they shut up, like someone had wound rubber bands around their little beaks. Total silence.

My jaw dropped. In a mere 24 hours the parents had apparently taught the nestlings to understand that I might represent danger! I hadn't heard any warning as I made my way to the tree.

I suspected the nestlings were red-naped sapsuckerettes, so I scoured the Internet for the parental warning cry. There I bumped into information on the yellow-bellied sapsucker. Uh oh.

My wobbly scarlet ibis narrative fell apart. Red-naped and yellow-bellied sapsuckers had been classified as one. Curiously, the description of the red-naped at no point says it has red on its nape. The yellow-bellied has red completely surrounded by black.

So my unusual "red-naped" was actually a common yellow-bellied sapsucker, *Sphyrapicus varius*, properly in its home range, but not exotic. Oh darn. Good thing I wasn't in the wild trying to differentiate between, say, a black bear and a grizzly. Still lovely.

Renewed lesson No. 1: Haste makes waste.

Nevertheless, the episode of sudden silence of the nestlings sticks in my mind, and I smile every time I think of it. It intrigued and amazed me, evoking lesson No. 2: how marvelous and miraculous nature is, in all its subtleties.

Some Kind of Love Story

The gander remembered the day he found her. He was leading a leisurely V of geese across the leaden skies. They were caravanning the heavens by day.

Hundreds of feet below him the great prairie and trees spread out, a checkerboard of browns, golds, greens, and the rainbow colors of the roofs of the houses the people occupied. He was studying the peculiar way people walk when he heard her voice.

She was honking with the joy of flight, the joy of the cool fall air whistling through her wings; the joy of living. He caught her eye. She smiled, slowed and honked louder. He grew warm inside.

All that day and the next and the next she moved up closer to him every time they took the air after gorging themselves in the fields and then resting in the lakes. Now, just by turning his head slightly, he could see her flapping steadily along just behind him. Her voice, pure and sweet as the spring water they drank steadied him. Her presence comforted him.

Later they would gaze at each other, resting their heavy bodies in the stubble fields as the last rays of the sun disappeared behind the dark hills, tinting the clouds pink.

He thought she was the most beautiful Canada goose he had ever seen--her head black as anthracite, her cheeks white as the snow they had fled, her slim neck like a supple rod of carved ebony.

The goslings born to them grew strong and sleek as their parents, with powerful wings and black webbed feet. After a few years the gander looked proudly as they flew realizing that nearly the entire V was of the same family of Canada geese--*Branta canadensis*. His family.

When he watched them undulate silently and regally across the fall skies, they did not look like merely common geese.

As usual, the gander thought, they were migrating from their nests on the lake shores and coastal marshes in northern Canada to their warmer winter grounds along the gulf of Mexico, some 4,000 miles as the crow--or goose--flies, flying at day, flying at night, because of the hunters spread up and down the land like different colored moving light bulbs. He led them, sighting their way south by the gleam of the pale moonlight off the lakes and ponds, and their infallible internal radar.

He was an old goose now. But he had never forgotten Minnesota because that was where he met his mate. His heart beat faster every time he passed the lakes that dotted the open prairies and farms.

The day was drizzly and cold, but as he peered over his shoulder on his right where she was honking cheerfully, and his left, where the line of their children stretched back, his heart grew warm. What could be better? He was with the ones he loved, and flying over the land most precious to him. His life had been full and good.

A warmth emanated up to him. He felt it every time he passed over Minnesota, and his mate did too. They must be good people who live there, he thought, to give off so much warmth.

He was thinking if he died right then he would have seen nothing except happiness, and what could be better than to die over the land you most loved? Just then his mate cried out in pain, her graceful wings crumpling. About the same time he heard the shot.

She turned head-over-heels, somersaulting toward the earth. He motioned for his strong young son to take the lead of the V.

He turned back, honking a final farewell to the V. He saw the shapes of people rushing toward his mate's limp body on the ground. He pirouetted on the air, his five-foot wings spread.

I'll stay with you, he honked as one of the men raised his shotgun.

Saga of a Reptile

One day while houseboating on the St. Johns River in Florida, I was astonished at the number of pieces of old tires that had been tossed willy-nilly onto the banks in this otherwise pristine wilderness area. We were cruising in the middle under low power, drifting with the current, observing from a distance the rampant growths and dead trees along the verge of the river. It was so wild and jungly-looking that several Tarzan movies had been filmed here.

I wondered if the movie people had been that messy. Or were Floridians that unconcerned about their waterways? Or both? Why would tires be needed here in the outback?

And then a tire unwound, and a 10-foot-long alligator slid menacingly down the bank and into the water. I shivered. If I had somehow been ashore, exploring, curious, naive. I shuddered.

At first glance the napping alligators on the bank looked like old tires, and I wondered why people had flung tires in the wilderness.

To add to my uneasiness, we moored in a little backwater. At 3 AM, in pitch darkness, I awoke to an anguished animal scream, a struggling splash--then sudden silence. The screech had been cut off as though a soundproof door had been slammed shut.

I slept uneasily. Could alligators clamber aboard houseboats and gnaw on unsuspecting guests?

My first contact with an alligator was years ago in a big box store with a scrabbling mass of baby cold-blooded beasts crawling over each other in an aquarium. I plucked one out, and for two dollars, along with an information card--"How to take care of your new pet," brought it home with me. Not thinking much about the future. It was just under eight inches long, snout to tip of tail.

He was a striking little creature, with orange slashes on its head above its eyes, dark green with yellowish stripes across its back, and mottled side with a yellowish-white stomach.

Alligators, *alligatoridae mississippiensis,* generally do not eat or bite straight ahead as we and many animals do, the information sheet said. They snap toward the side, possibly because of the location of their eyes atop their head.

Their biting muscles are exceptionally powerful, but the jaw-opening muscles are weak so adult humans can hold the jaw shut. When transported, duct tape is used around the jaws, *Wikipedia* says.

I had no such problems with my little eight-incher. At home I offered the blank-eyed reptile raw hamburger. He ignored it. Feeding directions said to force the mouth open, drop in food, and use the alligator fork--AKA as a pencil eraser--and shove it past the flap at the back of its throat. Alligators also get acid reflux. (What do they use for antacids?) I also fed it minced ham, sausage, and once poked a Cheerio down the esophagus, to no visible effect.

Eventually my brother in high school wanted the little alligator. His goal was for Allie to grow 10 feet long, put it on a leash, and lead it around our little town so it could snarf up all the little yapping dogs.

Never happened. When it was 14 inches long, Daryl's friend was playing with Allie, holding him in his palm. Allie promptly walked off the friend's hand, fell, and cracked his head on the basement's cement floor. And died.

Our funeral was as cold-blooded as the reptile itself. One long flush.

Cormorants Come Home

In my journal 45 years ago I wrote: *A dark lanky bird the size of a vulture struggled in the frothy water near the spillway of the Balta dam near where I lived. It disappeared under the water. How could I save it? Only by sliding down the steep bank on my butt, and plopping into the murky deep water. But no, I couldn't swim. I searched for a branch, or anything to help that poor bird. But no luck.*

Then it amazed me by popping up, flinging out dozens of droplets of water that gleamed like diamonds in the sunlight. Next, a real surprise, the bird flipped a wriggling minnow into the air, snatched it in his orange beak, and gulped it down.

I was taken aback. Obviously it didn't need help at all. What kind of bird was it? I'd never seen one before. For an hour I leaned back against the cold concrete spillway wall, watching it flip more minnows up and grabbing them in its curved-edge bill on their way down, as though to entertain me.

After a while the bird stood on a rock in a sunny place, spread its wings, and held them wide open for a long while. As though drying them. Why? That made no sense. Why not simply fly away so the moving air dried them?

Ducks and other waterfowl didn't need to dry their wings. When I'd hunted ducks, even after they'd just risen to the surface after diving, their entire bodies wet, including the wings, they took to the air. And if this big bird couldn't fly with wet wings, it would be in grave danger, hugely vulnerable to enemies.

It was an ugly bird too, I thought.

That night I paged through **Birds of North America** *(no internet in those days,) until bingo! I stumbled onto a picture of the bird: A double-crested cormorant. Which I'd never heard of. Or seen before. Thus at first I thought maybe it had been blown off course into our area by a storm, like the bird in a short story I taught,* "The Scarlet Ibis." *And the bird reference book said cormorants lived all over the United States. Surprised bird-lover me.*

A couple of days later that information was verified, as suddenly four cormorants showed up at the spillway. I watched them disport in the black water, diving, disappearing for up to a minute, and reappearing, sometimes with greenery draped on their necks like victorious garlands, sometimes flipping up little finnies and gulping them down, sometimes empty-mouthed. They possessed a certain grace. Especially with minnows wriggling in their beaks.

A few weeks ago Nikki and I were driving on a country road south of Rockville past a lake with a group of big dark lanky birds on a small island. I whipped out my camera, and took several shots of the two-foot-high birds. Gorgeous birds!

And then I recognized them. Cormorants! Not ugly at all. But beautiful. Because they weren't sopping wet? I discovered their feathers prevent air bubbles from getting trapped so the wings are easily waterlogged, allowing them to dive deep for prey, up to 26 feet down. And then they needed to be dried

Amazing the gifts nature offers us. All we have to do is receive them. Even if it sometimes takes many years.

Nikki and I found these cormorants alongside the road one day while we were driving in a rural area.

The Spring Peepers

Spring is most certainly the time of miracles, and there is no greater miracle than the peepers. It is the peepers, *pseudacris crucifer*-- tiny one-inch frogs that we hardly ever see--that truly announce the arrival of spring. To us their machinations seem a prodigious undertaking: lying in the mud below the slowly-thawing ice, while possibly being partially frozen, they measure the maximum temperature, the minimum temperature, and just how long that maximum temperature has been maximum. When all is right, they release a bubble of air from their throats, and on a cool spring-remindful evening we hear their cries echoing across the marshes and meadows.

Last night I went out to partake of that spring bonanza. Across the street from where I live is a lagoon that harbors hundreds, perhaps thousands, of the green or brown amphibians. With a couple of stars beginning to peer out, I neared the lagoon to the wild chorus of those little peepers. Darkness was filtering down through the sky as I stepped up to within a foot of the shore. Hearing the crunch of my shoes on the dead grass, half of the chorus held back, perhaps searching for the proper notes on another page of their choir book.

But the other half continued their serenade for me.

For a few minutes I stood there, still as a stone, and slowly the rest of the chorus began chirping in. Until finally their rusty cries echoed and echoed across the lagoon and into my ears, rattling my eardrums. Just a couple of feet in front of me I heard one peeping fearlessly, and as I strained through the dark, I fancied I could see it. There, crouching just beneath a broken-off reed. Isn't that the bottom of its mouth that is moving, filling slowly with air, then croaking?

Perhaps. But that wasn't important. There was other business on my mind. How is it, I wondered, these little beasts can so accurately predict the correct time for themselves to climb out of their estivation and into life again? It is absolutely necessary for them, of course, because a mistake means a cold death. But how do they do it?

It is, of course, a mystery humankind will probably never solve, like other unknowable mysteries of nature. But it always makes me think. We feel we are the rulers of the earth, and that the animals are the subservient creatures, but out there in the wilds are untold billions of little one-inch creatures who more accurately than you or I have figured out exactly when spring has arrived, exactly when it is safe to move out into the cool water, exactly the time when they should inflate the skin at the bottom of their jaws and slowly expel it, peeping and croaking.

If these frogs weren't peeping and croaking now, it would definitely mean something: that spring had not officially arrived, no matter the date on the Gregorian calendar, which we take to mean something merely because the word "spring" is stenciled on one of those days.

To me the peeping and croaking--the high and low ribbits, seemingly led by one frog with others following just behind, as though practicing the "words" the leader had said--is a reminder of yet how little we know about nature, and how much, in the end, we are at its tender mercy.

Revenge in the Bird Kingdom

One day while walking to the Rockville post office, we spotted a hawk in middle of a side street, standing on hot macadam 30 feet away, looking angry and perplexed. Though slim, it seemed large and imposing, perhaps 16 inches tall, and it glared at us as we walked by, but didn't move.

I hurried back for my camera, hoping the gorgeous brown bird would still be there. Five minutes later, I was surprised to find it in the same spot.

As I snapped away, I noticed the hawk did not have any prey clamped in its talons, a logical reason why it would be on the ground. So what was it doing here?

The family *Accipitridae*, or hawks, contains 208 species worldwide, from eight to 48 inches long, and from three ounces (the sharp-shinned hawk) to 20 pounds (the harpy eagle of Mexico).

Hawks possess keen color vision, almost as keen as that of the unparalleled vision of eagles, which allows hawks to spot rodents from on high and dive down from their soaring perch to scoop up dinner. Their large eyes are incapable of rotating, so to look from side to side, they have to turn their heads.

This Cooper's hawk didn't move, practically posing for me, until I adjusted a camera setting, and it flew. No more pictures, I figured. But it landed on a shepherd's crook in a nearby garden.

Using a maple trunk as cover, I crept closer until I could slowly rise and shoot through the Y of the tree. Despite the clicking of the shutter, the hawk seemed unaware of me. Or unconcerned.

As it sat on the shepherd's hook, it closed its eyes as a breeze ruffled its breast feathers. It wobbled momentarily.

At that moment I noticed a strange phenomenon: a stream of little brown birds was streaking in from all directions into two large maples above me, ferociously chittering and cheeping. With the hawk's eyes closed, and under cover of the cacophony, I moved closer, snapping pictures, until I stood about 10 feet away.

A minute later the hawk opened its eyes, dropped to the ground, and stood in the soft dirt amidst the leaves of a potato plant, alternately glaring at me and looking confused. Obviously ill.

Meanwhile, at least a hundred little brown birds in the trees were going wild with ecstasy. Their cheeps and chitterings were filled with rejoicing as they darted wildly from branch to branch. They knew something was amiss with their mortal enemy, and they were making fun of the big bad raptor.

I felt sorry for it, and back home, called our local raptor person. But by the time I returned to find a way to bring the bird to her, the hawk was gone.

So too were the little brown birds, and the hot noon air remained deathly silent.

This Cooper's hawk was sick when I found it and took this photo.

A Notable Daytime Visitor

Usually I enter my office gingerly, not wanting to spook whatever is parading outside, gracing me with its presence. Chickadees, woodpeckers, squirrels, rabbits--the enchanting denizens of Mother Nature. Our yard has become a sort of Downton Abbey, the variegated animals like villagers depending on us for support.

The other afternoon I spotted the usual suspects--cardinals, jays, and a raft of LBBs, little brown birds. Three steps later I stopped with a jolt. Outside, 10 feet from my desk, feathery feet clamped onto a lilac branch, stood a great brown owl.

Weren't owls nocturnal? That's why the immense eyes, right? Nikki and I listed owls we knew--barn, snowy, great horned--I wasn't sure. Whatever, it was big. Twenty inches long, and stocky.

The bird books identified it as a barred owl, which has dark eyes. But hers (she looked femaleish) were slits in her round face so it was difficult to tell. As I snapped pictures, the owl remained silent and unmoving, while other birds chattered and flitted about.

Which gave me pause. Didn't owls lunch on little birds? Finally the great bird swiveled her head and opened her dark eyes as though to say, "Who, me?" My reference indicated barred owls eat mice, voles, snakes, frogs--and the kicker, "birds at your feeder."

So this did not seem tenable, antagonists admixing, some LBBs eating seeds, ignoring the owl, turning their backs, pecking away, chirping, having a high old time. A blue jay hopped onto suet three feet away. No reaction from either bird. Was the owl ill? Did the birds sense weakness?

For better photos, I stepped outside, to no discernible reaction from the owl. Her eyes remained closed, so I studied this beautiful raptor, grayish head, dark brown eyebrows, yellow beak, brown back with white bars, soft white and brown breast feathers.

She looked ancient and wise. Perhaps why a group of owls is called a wisdom, or a parliament?

Suddenly she pushed off--on wings four feet wide. Thrilling! I could hardly catch my breath as she flew away. Silently.

Ten minutes later, she returned, like a regular to the same church pew. She settled in and gazed at me, perhaps to report to her friends. "Hey Myrtle, you should see this guy. All day he sits at his desk and moves his fingers every once in a while. Really!"

She fluffed her feathers, scratched her neck with yellow talons, pecked her chest. She rotated her head seemingly 180 degrees, which behavior once led to the belief that if you walk around an owl, it will wring its own neck. Folklore says owls bring good or bad fortune, sickness or health, life or death. And hide by day as their beauty angers other birds.

She returned a final time the next day. Since then, during quiet times, I have glanced up into the lilac, wistfully wondering what happened to that amazing bird that brightened my life.

This barred owl spent two days
in a tree outside my window
and hasn't returned.

Touching Wildness

I've never held a live rattlesnake, though I've wanted to, and was close enough, but didn't, for obvious reasons. I tried to grab a tarantula when I was six, but a man in the Red Owl Store prevented me.

Having grown up surrounded by wild animals that I held--harmless caged chickens, doves, and rabbits--I suppose that transformed into a desire to make contact with real wild animals.

The first ones occurred while reading a paperback book and leaning back against a tree when I was 11. My non-book hand lay flat against the ground beside me. After a while I felt wriggling beneath my hand, and when I checked, saw a young garter snake crawling out of a hole in the ground. Instinctively I petted it--and then its six following brethren, without any reaction from them.

Snakes are not slimy, like many people think, but dry and smooth--or rough depending where you touch them. Their most salient feature is their muscularity. They are surprisingly strong. For several days afterwards I returned reading there, and saw and petted the survivors, until zero came up out of the hole.

On a blistering North Dakota summer day a red-winged blackbird coasted over our box elder tree and glided into the open door of the chicken coop, seeking coolness, I figured. My brother and I had been tasked with preventing our chickens from flying over the fence and escaping, a hot job we hated.

We raced into the coop, slammed the door, and when my eyes adjusted, I nabbed the bird. I petted it, and pronounced it beautiful--until it bit the skin by my thumb, drawing blood. Twice, quickly. I squealed both times.

I had caught many grasshoppers, which spit brown juice (a combination of partially-digested plant material and slightly acidic digestive enzymes) all over my hands, which made me look like I'd been working hard in the dirt. Or polishing shoes. I fed the grasshoppers to our cat, who sat on her haunches and held them between her front paws and crunched away.

Years later the North Dakota Badlands provided me with opportunities to touch wild animals. I had been driving on back roads in the South Unit of Theodore Roosevelt National Park when I came upon three feral horses. I stopped and rolled down the window to take a picture.

That seemed to be a signal to one to clip-clop closer until five feet away. I had been camping out, and had a box of Cheerios. I filled my palm with the little oats and offered them. The horse snorted at my movement, then moved slowly closer, until he saw the food and stuck his lips into my palm and gobbled up several Cheerios.

I was certainly cheered, feeling the touch of warm and damp lips on my palm. I did pat his nose for only a second before he jumped back. I refilled my palm, and eventually a second horse ate, but not the shy third.

At the same park decades later I stopped to observe a herd of bison who were meandering across the road. I rolled the window down to hear them better, and suddenly a massive male moved within a couple of feet of me, grunting deeply, scaring me. I was close enough to rub the rough fur on his hump--but chose not to. The beast after all weighed about 2,000 pounds.

I've had dragonflies land on my fingers, held downy woodpeckers, and rose-breasted grosbeaks after they smacked into our window, petted an opossum. During my life I've ridden an elephant, whose hair was sharp as a wire brush, picked up a harmless skink in the British Virgin Islands, and held mice.

One day I'd like to feel a shark, maybe ride an alligator, and swim with a dolphin. The lure of knowing more about wild animals is powerful.

In Fine Odor

Fetching the newspaper in the dark of morning, I smelled the skunk, and froze as its claws clicked down the steps. In the porch light its eyes flashed like new silver dollars before it ambled off, obviously unimpressed with me, mano-a-skunko.

That's because skunks possess no natural enemies, except the Great Horned Owl, which has almost no sense of smell.

I've gone one-on-one with skunks before. Years ago, half-blinded by the low sun as I jogged on a lonely trail, I didn't spot the skunk until it was 10 feet away, its maximum spraying distance.

The skunk planted its feet, staring, as if to proclaim "This is my trail, and just what are you going to do about it, huh?" Seconds later, I lofted a dirt clod to help it mosey along.

In one quick motion the skunk whirled, hoisted its tail, and sprayed. I jumped back, untouched physically by the cloud of floating droplets that glittered in the evening light like a trove of airborne diamonds, but touched emotionally. Gazing at the sparkling mist I could only shake my head in awe. Who would think a skunk could create anything so beautiful?

Several years later, I spotted three eight-inch kit skunks jumping on each other, rolling and romping like kittens. From the far side of my car, I shot photos of their frolics. They were alone.

Where was the protective mother?

Their joyful play lured me closer, across the yellow center line, nearer and nearer, always shooting, until I was 10 feet away.

Now the skunklets took me for a playmate. They charged with paws raised, darting back into the brush, jumping out sideways and skidding in puffs of dust before moving back into the cover.

They seemed harmless, so I concocted the bright idea of petting them to impress my friends--with photographic proof of my derring-do. The lead skunk gazed at me adoringly as I tried to reach down and touch its back, focus, and shoot. But without autofocus, it couldn't be done.

So I had another bright idea: I slipped off my shoe, and stuck out my foot. Using both hands to operate the camera, wobbling like a one-legged novice ballerina in a white sock, I petted their heads and striped backs with my toes, because the little beasts didn't stink. Probably too young to pack weaponry.

A dozen shots later, I was thrilled with undeniable evidence of my bravery.

Half a mile down the road I realized my mistake. In the open, their skunky odors evidently dispersed. In the enclosed car they did not. Coughing, eyes watering, I opened the windows. Little help.

Finally, I stopped and removed my shoes and socks, and piled blankets and tools on them in the trunk. Eventually they had to be destroyed.

But since I had achieved my goal of petting the little beasts, with photographic proof, I guess I didn't get skunked after all.

The Delight of Wild Creatures

The bald eagle squatting in a shorn alfalfa field 50 feet from the side of the road was definitely inhaling a snake, still squirming. Or did the eagle's eating make the snake seem alive? Finally only a couple of inches of the tail remained, which the eagle slurped down like a thick colored strand of spaghetti.

Viewing wild animals is a delight nature offers to me time after time when I'm driving, like spotting a wild fisher trot across the road, or a male pheasant slipping off into the weeds, or a dead tree trunk filled with painted turtles. I regularly revel in dozens of nature-related adventures.

One day a turkey vulture, an eagle-sized black bird whose job it is to clean up the detritus of animal bodies that cars smashed on the road. Vultures ride the thermals until their keen sense of smell detects a carcass, and then it's lunch time. I see them often, large and dark in the sky, and first think they are eagles. But then they flap, a dead giveaway, as eagles flap only to create lift, and then soar and glide. Vulture heads and faces are easily visible, and supremely ugly, but for a good reason: no feathers cover those areas so they can clean themselves easier, and we can see their dark red skin.

Painted turtles the size of a slice of bread also frequent the roads. I see them moving slowly onto the macadam, attempting to return home where they were born, and lay eggs.

I always stop to pick up the ones who have survived. They struggle a little in my hand, probably wondering what monster has gotten hold of them. The shells are cool and solid, the underbelly rich orange and greenish-yellow, with black lines. They seem ancient, so I wonder if I maybe slipped through a time portal back into the Cretaceous, and glance around for a *T. rex* or triceratops. Seeing none, I transfer the turtle across the road in the direction they were traversing, into the grass.

Not so with a huge rock of a snapping turtle I spotted one day on a side road, the first one I'd ever seen. I'd heard a lot about them, like they could bite through your finger with their thousand-pound bite force.

The snapper hissed at me, warning me not to come any closer. No problem. I shot several photos, but stayed far enough away not to get grabbed.

I feel true joy spending a few moments with these wild animals, and I am thrilled for hours afterwards every time I think of them. What could be more wonderful?

The snapper doesn't look too happy at my shooting photos of it.

The Squirrels and Me

My squirrels get along famously with me, stealing my black-oil sunflower seeds, sitting comfortably on a tray of seeds made only for birds. They get along famously with me, but I do not get along famously with them. The black ones are the most difficult.

I pound on the window with the edge of an old foot-long ruler, whacking away and yelling, "Get away from here! Go home! Not on my watch!" or other such inanities. Thankfully they do not maraud the suets, although I'm not here all the time and sometimes I'll catch one of the furry little rodents skittering up a branch and sniffing at one of them. But before he or she can take a chomp, I'm at my little metal-lined tool, and pound away.

Used to be that the squirrels would jump when I smacked on the window and speed away, their tails flailing. But now through the Law of Diminishing Returns, they might start a bit if they are facing away from me, or young unschooled ones might dart for a tree and climb just high enough so I can see them sitting in a crotch munching away on the sunflower seeds they've stolen.

I've seen YouTube videos that show how people have rigged up slings that will fling the squirrels flying through the air, making them flying squirrels even when they are not, but I don't think those would be very successful. A lot of time in the designing of them, perhaps some fun in watching the squirrels flung away, but afterwards the same result: they return, this time with in-laws that they don't like so they can convince them to hop into the sling for an amazing time, then chuckling when they are flung away. While the disoriented flying squirrels are recovering their wits, the older knowing squirrels are after the sunflower seeds.

So short of shooting them, I'm at a loss. I've tried live-trapping them, but my live traps are too small, I guess, borrowed, and it would cost a pretty penny to get larger ones, not to mention the gas to transfer them to their new homes in the country.

There are stories of dogs and cats moving across the country to find their masters months or even years later. My guess is that the same would hold true for these squirrels, because they are comfortable in my backyard, and are having a good time laughing at me and taking advantage of my largesse.

So I knew I needed a new gig. So now when squirrels pop into my view, I rap on the window like usual, scream and yell, adding a few curses, which seemed to work for a while, until the Law took effect again. One day I was very frustrated with the squirrels, especially the black ones, which merely glanced in my direction as I pounded on the window, and smiling as they dug into the sunflower seeds. That got my goat.

So I rushed out into our three-season porch, found a long stick, the handle off an old implement, opened the door and rushed out, smacking the stick against the green plastic chair just outside the door, yelling and screaming, chasing them over to trees that they fly up onto, and pounding the stick against the trees while channeling my inner Tarzan.

Most people who know me would consider me pretty calm, I think. They would be surprised to know that I smack the door open and jump outside and scream at the squirrels. The dog next door doesn't know what I'm yelling at, so he barks and increases the cacophony. I noticed that the kids at recess at the John Clark Elementary School next door, just beyond the tennis courts perhaps 200 feet away, stopped their play one day and looked in my direction.

So I have to thank the squirrels for helping me take my life in another direction, channeling my inner Tarzan.

Pirates on Lake Superior?

The gray band of the Milky Way, dimmed by the yellow scimitar of the moon, had sent me yawning to bed in the bow of our 32-foot sailboat, the Pearl. The gentle pitter-patter of the rain augmented the peace, and I dropped off until a barred owl screamed twice, high to low, "yowwwww," and a minute later another beast shrieked once in pain, then was silent.

We were moored 24 miles from civilization, anchored a hundred yards off Outer Island, as far into Lake Superior as the Apostle Islands extend. The waves were lapping and burbling against the hull. All else was silent except for the occasional snort of one of my sleeping compatriots, and the whine of a single elusive mosquito that had drilled me twice, escaped, and was laying in wait for its next chance.

It was 2:30 AM, and the darkness was complete when I first heard the diesel engine of a boat idle by. Maybe that had awakened me. A minute later, it returned, the sound louder, then fading. A moment later, it came back past us again, and then back the other direction.

Which made me suspicious. Was it checking us out? I switched on a light so they wouldn't think whoever it was that they could clamber aboard without resistance, because I feared that's what they were planning as I listened to it make trips five, six, seven.

So I woke our captain. He listened to the boat and peered out a porthole, catching a glimpse of light. But that was all. By this time everybody was awake, listening, wondering why a strange boat with was cruising back and forth nearby with no running lights.

We began to speculate why: Laying nets? Night fishing? Waiting for a signal from ashore? Picking up contraband from Outer Island? Building courage for boarding us?

Peering out into the blackness, all we could see was the faint glimmer of our "anchor light," high above on the mast as we swung gently on a single anchor back and forth on the breeze.

We'd come out into the Superior wilds to bid goodbye to a friend moving to Japan, as well as solve several of the world's pressing problems. That afternoon we had swum ashore in the icy water, someone saying, "It's like diving into ice cream," searched for agates and other colorful stones on the beach, endured a constant deluge of black flies and mosquitoes, ate lake trout, shared life histories, told stories, laughed, even cried--isolated from cell phones, computers, and televisions, sustained by our thoughts and our friendships, dependent only on ourselves for excitement. Until the pirates--or drug runners--contemplated boarding us.

That's what I was worried about.

After observing where the mystery boat was plying its wake--on the port, or left side, of our boat, which was nearest to Outer Island--the concept began to break down, because we were so close to the island. The boat would have to be running over sand and rocks and downed trees.

I had noticed how unnaturally quickly the engine noise of the intruder faded, then suddenly grew louder at times.

About 15 minutes later we figured out the answer: it wasn't another boat. No pirates or drug runners, nothing sinister, unless wind rippling through the rigging, sounding to everyone aboard exactly like an idling diesel engine, is sinister.

I took a lot of good-natured ribbing for "Bill's pirates" for the next two days. But that's the lot of a sometimes-fiction writer with a wild imagination.

Taking Pictures of God

I had just sprawled full-length across the rip rap rocks along the shore of Devils Lake when a car pulled up behind my white van on the side road above me. A woman in the passenger seat rolled down her window.

"Catching any fish?" She asked.

I held my camera up high. "Only fishing with my camera," I said, smiling.

The woman turned and said something to her husband. I thought they'd pull away, so I scootched down deeper into the rocks, feeling them press into my internal organs as I oriented my eyes to focus my camera on a close-up of a foxtail plant. I heard steps crunch on the gravel, and when I glanced up, a late-middle-aged man stood looking down at me.

"Catch any fish?" He said, oddly the same question as his wife. Seemed he should see I had no fishing gear. He shielded his eyes from the bright sun.

I shook my head and held up my camera again. "Only catching photos," I grinned. He stood, arms akimbo. The water from the giant lake lapped softly on the shore.

I asked, "You a fisher?"

He shook his head. "Haven't fished in 35 years. Just wanted to see what kind of fish you were catching this end of the lake. No fish, ha?"

"No," I replied. "Just pictures."

"Pictures, huh?" He said. "What's there to take pictures of?"

I was getting irritated now, because the longer I lay there without getting the picture the more uncomfortable I was becoming. The rocks were cold, hard and difficult to negotiate. I ached, and I was getting grouchy. I didn't want to get up without snapping the picture, because I'd have to replicate the painful process again later. I was no longer a spring chicken. But I didn't want to be uncivil.

"Pictures, huh?" He said. "What's there to take pictures of?"

He scowled when he looked at the rocks, the sparse growth of plants, the dead trees and brush in the lake. "The rocks? The weeds? The brush?" He said disdainfully. His swooping arm encompassed everything, even the impossibly-blue sky.

His attitude angered me. How could he not see all the beauty around him?

"Yes," I agreed, "the rocks, the weeds, the brush. And God."

He looked at me. "God?"

"Yes, I'm taking pictures of God," I said, and when I voiced it for the first time, I knew it was true.

He snorted. "I heard stories about the devil around here, but not God."

He meant how whites named the lake in 1884, misinterpreting the Santee Sioux's name for the waters--Spirit Lake--to refer to the devil. When the city and lake were officially named, a local preacher took the lead. "We will prove," he howled, "that Satan does not own this lake or this city!" Thus Devils Lake without an apostrophe.

I tried to explain to the man that as I photographed, the warmth of God's arm lay across my shoulders in the rays of the sun, his voice spoke in the wind sifting through the small branches and the plants along the shore, his face was upon the waters and the reflections of the sky and clouds on the surface. Most of all, I saw God's handiwork in the finally-wrought detail of each plant that I shot with my macro lens.

The man snorted again, and his wife yelled down to him. He whirled and seconds later I heard his car whining away down Highway 20. After I snapped the foxtail waving in the wind, I pushed myself up and sat on a warm rock, gazing out at the great Lake. I thought about the man and what he was missing in life by refusing to see the beauty around him. He was probably the kind of person who thinks driving through North Dakota (or South Dakota, or Saskatchewan) is one long bore. You find what you seek.

But then I realized I shouldn't be so hard on him. I had once been like him, until eventually I began to see the beauty of nature everywhere. Maybe something would trigger that impulse in him. Possibly even our interaction today.

As I climbed over the rocks on the rise to my van, I wondered about the couple and their strange behavior. At my vehicle I discovered the answer. My passenger-side door on the far side of the unlocked vehicle was open an inch or so, and I knew I hadn't used that door at all. Maybe they worried I would know the sound of my van's door closing?

Luckily I'd had nothing valuable in the van, and nothing was missing.

Except their morality.

And sense of what can be beautiful.

I was laying on these rocks when the couple began talking to me.

Even dead trees make beautiful shots by Devils Lake.

When the Earth Moved

Ernest Hemingway claimed that if a person was extremely lucky, the earth would move once, twice, or maybe three times during their lifetime. Thus I am extremely lucky--or easily moved--as I have been gifted with having the earth move many times during my life, each time filling me with a sense of awe, wonder, and majesty.

Most times the moves have involved animals, like seeing a doe flinging up silver jewels of water from her muzzle into sunlight; or noting a dragonfly, clutching the end of my finger, its head jerking robotically as its huge eyes examined me as though to say, "The guys'll never believe what I caught!"; or a Vee of trumpeter swans soaring low over me, their undersides pure white against the impossibly blue sky, while several honked to make sure I would perceive their beauty.

But the greatest instance occurred one day when I was cruising a highway that pierces the great Canadian wilds north of Winnipeg. Late afternoon shadows were flowing into early evening, and wraiths of mists were seeping out from under the kelly-green pines and curling across the tarred cracks in the highway. The mists and shadows twined together, like spirits. They swirled around trees, and into the primeval forest, like playing hide and seek. Nothing else moved in the great misty stretches of the wilderness.

Until I sped around a long curve. There, jowls swinging, walked a huge moose, with racks branching like brown lightning against the sky. My tires screeched as I hit the brakes. The moose strode onto the road, now only 10 feet in front of my car. Parts of his antlers were green.

In a sudden last ray of sunlight, he was reflected on the hood of my car. His thigh muscles rippled as he paraded in front of me. Over the purring of the engine and the thumping of my heart I heard the clop clop of his hooves on the pavement, as though a giant pair of hands--God's perhaps--applauded its beauty.

The moose stepped into the ditch, which seemed filled with mist thick as cream until it reached nearly level with the highway. The moose crossed the road--he stopped and looked at me to make sure I realized whose road it was, then angled down the ditch with a surety that said, "I know this land."

Then, except for his great head and antlers, he disappeared into the whiteness and began to run, appearing bodiless, the skull bobbing up and down. A hundred feet further he climbed easily up the other side of the ditch and on the threshold of the forest, turned to eye me, as though to say goodbye, and good riddance.

Then he shook his head and turned into the gathering gloom, and was swallowed by the trees.

I pulled over and suddenly found myself outside racing down the road and down into the soupy-white ditch, my body becoming mostly invisible, and up the other slant, hoping to see his form in the dark haze. At the verge of the trees, my shoes and face wet, I peered into the darkness of the pines. But he was gone. The breeze blew in my face, and I smelled the primeval forest, and perhaps the spoor of the moose.

I spotted one of his prints etched in the soft soil of the earth. I knelt and laid my hand in the large footprint easily, and felt it. I closed my eyes and inhaled, lifting my head. And the very earth moved.

The core of my being, the very center of my essence palpitated with the awe and wonder and mysteries of nature.

First moose I ever saw, in Canada.

The Gift

My most meaningful contact with a coyote occurred in a cove in Nevada, while contemplating my future with a very difficult new editor of a magazine I'd written for every month for years.

So my heart lifted when the coyote distracted me, trotting near the top of the butte above our houseboat. She moved in her domain, loose-limbed and confident. Her long black shadow pulsed against the rock face, similar to my pulsing thoughts, I reflected.

Hidden by a tamarisk, I studied her flashing legs, darting eyes, and sense of serenity in the desert, and simplicity of her life. Tonight she would raise her muzzle and howl, and relatives far away would echo her cry, while I tried to decide: money or self-respect?

She stopped and sniffed the air, her whiskers quivering. Had she smelled me? I'd just returned from a strenuous two-mile walk along a sand-bottom coulee up into the hills among geckos, birds, rocks, and creosote bushes, trying to sort out my thoughts.

Then the coyote surprised me: she stepped off the path. In the few days we'd shared our little inlet, she'd never stepped off the path. She ambled down a slab of rock towards the water. Thirsty?

Then I spotted a seagull on the shore, its great hooked beak and splayed toes spread possessively across the belly of a big carp. The coyote sauntered at the gull, tossing her head, nostrils dilating.

The gull raised its white head, glared at the interloper, and spread its wings. Preparing to flee, I thought, intimidated by the bared teeth of the advancing coyote.

Instead, the gull rushed the coyote, stopping 10 feet away, repeatedly jabbing its beak at the beast, croaking a harsh warning. "I won't be bullied. I won't give up my supper without a fight."

The coyote seemed unconcerned. She sniffed and stepped closer. Again the gull rushed and pecked and squawked angrily. The coyote jumped back, yawned, then calmly lay on her stomach, eyes fixed on the carp.

After a macho minute, the gull lowered its wings, and sidled back to its catch, pecking and tearing and gulping, keeping a wary eye on the coyote.

For 20 minutes the standoff continued, until the coyote seemed to sigh, rose, and turned away onto her regular path. The battle was over.

I released my pent-up breath, staring where the coyote had disappeared. I felt different. Relieved. The weight had dropped off my shoulders, thanks to the drama, the gift of the standoff between the coyote and the gull.

Now I knew what I had to do: stand my ground. Challenge my editor's bullying. Stick up for myself. Reclaim my self-respect. I had to step off my old path.

I sat on the ground as the air cooled and the bright moon rose, my arms wrapped about my knees, thinking how gifts come to us in many guises.

Just then, I heard faint yips rise into full-throated howls, and then the distant answers. I shivered as chills ran up and down my back. Up and down my spine.

Strength of the Land In Me

If you are lucky, you will find a piece of land you like; if you are fortunate, you will stumble upon a few acres that make you happy: if you search with determination and are blessed, you will discover a parcel of land to make your very soul sing.

I cannot tell you down which yellow-striped snake of highway my land lies. The telling, you see, would mean its certain ruination, just as the too-sudden opening of secrets from a lover's heart.

No, I cannot tell you other than to inform you it lies to the south and then west of me, grandly within the country, a plot of virgin soil never bitten by the sharp plow, a place I had begun to despair of ever finding.

And now like a happily-married man viewing a bachelor friend, I urge you toward a spouse of land in the hopes your betrothal to it might be as pleasurable and successful as mine. There is a tract of land out there just waiting to please, to cherish, you.

I found my land on a cold day late in the fall. The sky had been grayer than usual in my life that fall, the sun dimmer, the wind colder, the land bleaker, the thorns on the brush sharper. My eye had caught the feeble glimmer of the sun's rays against a lake a quarter-mile off-road. As I struggled through the dead prairie grasses clutching at my ankles, I carried a bulging gunny sack of problems slung over my shoulder.

But to cross the loose strands of rusty barbed-wire fence, I needed to lay those problems down. I stepped over the wires. Ah. The din of my mental battles subsided.

A few steps further and my world changed. Arrowing specks of geese honked their happiness of flight in the bright sky while a yellow-shafted flicker drummed on the hollow corpse of a tree, then flitted off to another. Something was afoot in this land, something that straightened my shoulders, brightened my eyes, quickened my step, warmed the icy spots in in my heart even as the temperature around me dropped. Though I had never set foot on this land before, I felt a camaraderie with it. The land and I struck up an instant friendship, borne of the rapport of a chemistry little seen and less understood.

I wandered the land; touching the American elms and cottonwoods and paper birch; inhaling the death of summer and the dusty dryness of fall; hearing the trickle of the rill over stones while far out on the lake a duck quacked its greeting; tasting a dead stalk of grass clipped between my teeth; seeing the golden setting sun spatter the sky pink, and a few lazy clouds, orange.

I was not in the looking when I found my land. But now I visit at least weekly, watching the seasons working their wonders across it. At times I lean against a tree on a hill overlooking the beaver dam, studying the beavers as they careen down their mud slides into their private lake; or I listen to the leaves rustle and murmur to themselves; or a I snap pictures of toadstools or mushrooms who pose for me.

My spot of land is always different each time I am there, and yet the same. When I need comfort or consolation the land welcomes me. When I rejoice, the very blades of grass in my parcel of land rejoice with me. It is forever summer when I'm on this land.

On a bright, cold day a month later I took the land to wife. I had come to the land with the intention of enfolding its charms in my arms, but the dainty trail of a weasel in the dusty snow, the beseeching black fingers of the trees etched against the blue sky while the breeze caressed my reddening cheeks, overcame any opposition I might have had.

In a daze I wandered the land, studying the nest of the red-tailed hawk, visiting a venerable bearded tree, feeling something growing inside me nearly to bursting. An hour later in the chapel-like stillness beneath the dome of tree branches above, I took the hand of the land in trade for my heart.

As though in agreement, the wind began sighing through the trees as I struck the bargain, seeming to say, "At last you have found us, and we have found you."

And now the strength of the land is within me. I am more than myself. I am back where we who grew to adulthood under the aegis of time outdoors in our childhood lands, belong: back home again, back on the land.

Even though no registrar of deeds has my name printed anywhere in his files as owning this land, yet this parcel of land belongs to me as surely as the breath of air I am now inhaling. I have given something to this tract of land that no one else can give-- the distinctness of my personality--and she has given me much in return.

And now I urge you to search for a piece of land to call your own, a place where you are accepted for what you are, a place where you can put aside, for a happy while, life's problems.

Perhaps you don't want to give your heart to a piece of land. You might not wish to live for it. Ah, but the land does not mind. She does not mind if you are merely another person come to taste her sweetness.

So why now wander out and embrace that special part of your country in your arms? Get to meet her, eventually to know her. Eventually you may be allowed to plant a kiss or two, or maybe you will start a long and fine romance with your own little tract of land.

Life Changes

When I was 10 I throbbed with impatience waiting for the onset of the spring thaw so I could once more crawl around in the ravine in the empty lot across the street and excavate fossils from its layered walls. Especially those of *Tyrannosaurus rex*.

The Dakota winter was long, my imagination fevered, and it needed to be satisfied, so while the snow blew and temperatures dropped to -30, I read and reread Ray Bradbury's classic short story, "A Sound of Thunder," where through his words I stepped into an ancient hot jungle in which he described the *Tyrannosaurus rex* so perfectly it became real to me: *It came on great oiled, resilient, striding legs. It towered 30 feet above half of the trees, a great evil god, folding its delicate watchmaker's claws close to its oily reptilian chest. Each lower leg was a piston, a thousand pounds of white bone, sunk in thick ropes of muscle, sheathed over in a gleam of pebbled skin like the mail of a terrible warrior. And from the great breathing cage of the upper body those two delicate arms dangled out front, arms with hands which might pick up and examine men like toys, while the snake neck coiled. And the head itself, a ton of sculptured stone, lifted easily upon the sky. Its mouth gaped, exposing a fence of teeth like daggers. Its eyes rolled, ostrich eggs, filled with hunger.*

After reading those words I mentally harnessed up my pet *T. rex*, Tyranno. Climbing aboard, my legs clutched tightly around his muscular neck 20 feet above the ground, I rode like a great god. Together we stalked back and forth on the streets of Wishek, searching for tidbits for his insatiable appetite, like a 60-foot-long *brontosaurus* or a duck-billed *hadrosaur* for a series of lunches.

That helped. Nevertheless I ached for spring to dig out *T. rex* fossils and a positive identification from Nicholas Hotten III, Acting Curator at the Smithsonian Institution in Washington, D.C.

This is how I imagined my pet *Tyrannosaurus rex* Tyranno looked. (Photo Credit to Jcoope12 at Pixabay.)

But finding *T. rex* fossils never happened. I knew nothing about them, where they might be found, how big they were, anything. But because I was finding fossils in the empty lot, it seemed logical that I would also find *T. rex* fossils. Fun to pretend, living in a make-believe world, leaving boyish troubles behind.

Out of that fascination grew my lifetime hobby of a love of dinosaurs. Say "dinosaurs" and those classic names come to mind and roll trippingly off the tongue, while their images blossom in the brain: *brontosaurus, stegosaurus, triceratops, allosaurus*--and of course the terrible tyrant himself, *Tyrannosaurus rex*. All constant and unchanging for the past 60 years amidst a world of whirling change.

A *brontosaurus*, which I imagined my pet Tyranno could catch and eat. Note the *triceratops* in the background. (Credit Pixabay.)

Or so I thought. Whoops! Suddenly I discovered the world of dinosaurs has changed. One new dinosaur is being discovered every week now, including recent tyrannosaurs named *Yulang* and *Yutranno*. Their discovery has altered the dinosaur world forever.

These *tyrannosaurs*, still vicious top-of-the-food-chain monsters--*Yutranno* was 30 feet long--were buried millions of years ago in minutes by volcanic debris, preserving their soft organs and scaly skin. And their feathers.

Yes, feathers. Which means their cousin *T. rex* also bore feathers, probably on the top of its head, upper back, and tail, the experts say.

This discovery has turned my dinosaur world topsy-turvy. Dinosaurs with feathers lose all their powerful cachet, like a white shark with gums and no teeth. What's next? *T. rexes* as vegetarians, gobbling sphagnum moss and fiddlehead ferns?

I've always been a dreamer, so I think I'll immerse myself in my myriad old dinosaur books where *T. rexes* are *T. rexes*, and rule their Cretaceous world as they always have, with unadulterated speed, and force--and no feathers.

Getting Rid of Rocks

When I was a kid, my mother must have quailed when she washed my hand-me-down jeans in her wringer washer. One time when I was 7 and she was out hanging a load on the clothesline, I tossed a pair of jeans into the washer. When she returned and put the pants through the ringer, it ground and screeched and Mom was not happy. She had to work to get the wringer working again.

She said, "I told you to empty the pockets before you threw your pants into the washer!"

"I thought I did."

She pulled rocks out of both front pockets, and held them in her palms, showing them to me. A couple were broken, and a pants pocket was torn.

"Um, I guess I must have forgot."

I have always loved rocks, searching for attractive ones in the gravelly streets of Wishek or crawling around on a couple of huge piles of various-sized pebbles to palm-sized rocks at Wishek Concrete and Lumber Products three blocks away, searching for any colorful pieces, shiny lumps of quartz, and especially agates, which were rare and difficult to find.

One day in sixth grade the father of a classmate drove us out to a place called Fossil Butte 20 miles away, a 200-foot-high hill that I'd never heard about. On the slope huge rocks the size of cars lay in various places, as though plopped down from the sky. While our driver stretched out to nap in the back of the station wagon, we kids began to search the huge rocks, made up of layers of shale.

As we broke the layers apart, we uncovered dozens of ancient fossilized ferns, looking as though they had seemingly been scratched into the gray surface of the shale with a very fine black magic marker. We also found ancient leaves, perfectly-preserved shape-wise, other small plants, an occasional shell, and a couple of five-inch-long skeletons of fish.

Treasures in my mind. I was delighted. I piled my gifts in my pockets until they could hold no more, and took them home as souvenirs, putting them in a shoebox so I could examine them when I wanted to.

The next year we moved into a huge square house kitty-corner from an empty lot and brought the shoebox with me. I was more than delighted to discover every type of rock I could imagine existed in that empty lot, occasional agate pebbles through fist-sized fossils, Indian arrowheads and flint hide scrapers or knives, and great rock hammers half the length of a loaf of bread, and as thick.

I soon filled several shoeboxes in our basement bedroom where I could admire, play with, make up stories about, and show them off to friends and classmates.

Eventually Mom wanted them out of the house. Where should I put them? Our chicken coop was our only other building, so I lugged them out and slid them into an opening just above ground in the back of the chicken coop. Then I went away to college, started teaching, and forgot about the rocks, as I just didn't have time to think about them.

When my stepdad died and mom decided to sell the house, I returned to help, and remembered the boxes of relics. Though I had done nothing with them during busy college years and my first two years of teaching, I felt the desire returning. I decided to procure them and take them with me to Pettibone, where I was teaching.

I reached under the chicken coop in a spot where I'd set them in a heavy cardboard box, but touched nothing. On my knees I couldn't see them. Nor with a flashlight. They were gone. I felt sick. Some people had known they were there. So who took them? I never had the slightest idea.

Yet all the rock-gathering of those early years precipitated in me a continued love of rocks as an adult, digging at supervised dinosaur sites in Wyoming and North Dakota, finding arrowheads, flint pieces and fossils in fields to increase my supply, examining rocks in museums, and searching in front of a dam for Jesus rocks only half an hour from where we live.

And found some of them. Every time yet today when I discover a worthy rock, I get excited again.

We traveled to the north unit of the Theodore Roosevelt National Park to spend time looking at the huge concretions there. Nikki and I have continued to dig dinosaurs at different sites in North Dakota--a different kind of rock--and will again this summer.

Recently I went through my shoeboxes of rocks, and decided to clean out many that aren't worth keeping. Some were easy to toss because they were small, but also because they didn't pull up any memories. But some were difficult to toss out.

I realized they still reminded me of parts of my own personal history, and deserved better than that. At least that's what I figured when I slid them back on the shelf.

Some concretions were massive.

Nikki stands among some huge concretions in the North Dakota Badlands of the north unit of Theodore Roosevelt National Park.

Trying To Fit In

One morning I slipped out of my dorm room bed early, and stumbled half-awake into the hall. Normally at this house I heard nothing, as I was an early riser, and college kids stayed up later.

Once out in the hall, I was surprised to hear faint sounds. Not a radio or record player someone might have left on. But a feeble voice.

Every day at this time I liked to think about calling pert and lovely Jane. From my stepdad I'd picked up the habit of lifting the receiver and dialing all the numbers except the final one in a difficult situation. I guess it made me feel that one time I would dial that last number too. But I couldn't now, as I had little money, zero wheels, and even less courage.

As I walked down the hall toward the phone booth and bathroom, the feeble cry increased. I couldn't make it out the words. Except they were repetitive.

The sounds grew louder, weak yelping like half-barks of a starving chihuahua, emanating from the lavatory or a nearby room. What could this be about?

I stopped at the lavatory door, and heard the sound come from inside. I pushed the door open, and the intensity of the cries rose into shouts.

"Finally finally finally," a voice croaked. "Help, help, help."

Four legs stuck out at varying angles from under a stall. What in the world?

Then I recognized two legs, belonging to Mack, Mr. miniscule from our dorm floor, who owned legs thin as piano wire.

And then I recognized the other legs: from Mack's massive friend, Cappy. I opened the stall door, and saw the dilemma-- unconscious Cappy lay sprawled atop Mack.

When I first heard the feeble voice my fertile imagination could have concocted 50 different possibilities of what could possibly have happened. Yet none of them would have been even closer to reality than the sun was to the earth.

I grunted as I tried to roll Cappy off Mack. But he was a really big guy, and I wasn't strong enough. Plus he stunk of vomited liquor, which wasn't inviting. I attempted to lift him, with the same result.

Mack kept saying, hoarsely, "Get him off me, get him off me."

"Be right back," I said.

"No," Mack said, "No, don't go. You won't come back."

He kept yelling as I went out the door. I hastened back to my room, woke my roommate, and explained what had happened, and after some effort he and I lifted dead-weight Cappy high enough for Mack to crawl out. I had to help him stand, because he was reeling as he looked down at Cappy.

"Is he--is he-- dead?" Mack asked.

I checked. "No," I said. "He's still breathing."

They had decided to get drunk together. Afterwards they returned to the dorm, talked, and had to go to the bathroom. Mack helped Cappy stagger to the commode. As Mack supported him, Cappy promptly passed out, knocked Mack down, and splayed him across the floor, laying on top of the lower half of his body. No matter how much Mack struggled, he couldn't get loose from under the behemoth.

Luckily Mack could still breathe. Several hours later I arrived at the scene.

I'd heard Mack and Cappy plan getting drunk several times before. Cappy was an American Indian from California, and Mack an Eskimo from Alaska. Both were out of their element.

That I understood. I had come to college from an unusual culture of the Germans from the Ukraine, and I didn't feel like I fit in either.

From knowing them, and this experience, I learned how difficult it is sometimes to fit in.

The Fullness of the Empty Lot

This piece was published in North Dakota REC Magazine in April 1989 and The Reader's Digest, October 1989.

In the muted light of the pigweed jungle, I scan the damp earth for my enemy's footprint. A canopy of leaves large as dinner plates shades me from the blazing sun.

There!

The faint impression of his heel. Senses humming, I stoop, eyes darting side to side in the gloomy silence. The insects pause from their interminable clicking and buzzing. Too quiet! My heart hammers. Slow as an hour hand I turn my head.

A flash of color! A scream! Too late!

I am knocked down. My enemy's weight squashes my shoulder into the mud. The edge of his soft pigweed blade presses into my neck.

He flings back his shaggy head and laughs. "You almost had me, Willy."

Now he is my best friend, Tom. "But you made one mistake."

He helps me up. "What?"

"The arrowheads in your pocket. They clink."

This skirmish was one of many that raged in the four-square-block empty lot across from our house. In my empty lot I was blessed with a vast forest of pigweed, a murky pond and a deep ravine. What I learned in school, or read about, I tested on the land in that lot.

Swatting down flying grasshoppers with stinkweed taught me lift, speed, trajectory, and physics: the weapon's mass against air resistance determined the energy needed to knock my prey down.

I discovered archaeology by digging up two arrowheads and a war ax with what looked like dried blood on one end. I uncovered flakes of worked flint, agates, and other rocks.

Also, I dug up dozens of small bones. Setting them into a sinuous curve, I exhibited the snake remains to my class. (Later the Smithsonian identified them as gopher.)

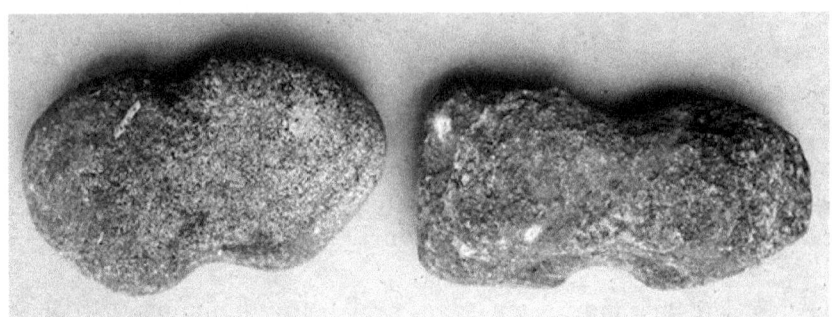

When I found these Indian-made items in the empty lot, I thought they were war axes--in reality they are mauls, or hammers.

This is the only photo I have of the area that affected my life so immensely, and shows only part of the empty lot across the street.

After spring thaw or summer thunderstorms the ravine frothed with cascading water filled with leaves and twigs, dead insects and animals. Each torrent gouged the ravine anew, creating a delta with pebbles arrayed larger to smaller: potamology, the study of rivers.

But the real gift, with mud oozing between my toes, was poring over the newly exposed strata. Levels of sediment--stratigraphy--were marked by distinct bands peppered with roots, beetle husks, small tunnels, different colors of soil, and rocks.

One day I pried out an apple-sized rock with knobs across its surface. Ancient shark teeth! I thought. I could hardly sleep waiting for the Smithsonian's answer. Their onionskin paper read, "Distal end of metapodial of *equus complicatus,* or ancient horse, adding that it "articulated fairly well with no. 8" of the 12 specimens I'd sent, which included a piece of skull of ancient bison and bone of an ancient camel. Nicholas Hotton III, Acting Curator, defined *distal* and *metapodial,* then added *All your specimens are from Pleistocene (Ice Age) deposits.*

Ice Age! References indicated glaciers a mile high had pressed down upon this very land! I was delirious with excitement and soon told everyone in town about my discoveries.

My interest piqued, my winter reading about Schliemann and Troy, Pompeii, Ancient Egypt, Rome opened up new worlds.

All because of the "empty" lot.

But from that parcel of land I learned so much more: a love of beauty, the triumphal joy of discovery, and awe of the intricate meshings which made that little world--and the big one--work. And most of all, to respect my own abilities. The empty lot was a microcosm of life; a practice field. I knew it intimately. I loved it desperately.

Sometimes when the ache is upon me, I might pass through a small town to search for an empty lot. I needn't drive up and down the streets; I merely need a minute to spot the dreamy eyes of the kids. Then I know that the lot, like Shangri-la, exists.

And I can find it and walk through its knee-high swishing grass once more.

www.ingramcontent.com/pod-product-compliance
Lightning Source LLC
LaVergne TN
LVHW010159070526
838199LV00062B/4416